Stock Trading for Beginners

The Easiest Step-by-Step Guide for Investing in Market Stock. The Most Important Tactics, Trends, and Strategies to Trade in Lucrative Way in Bad and Good Times

Table of Contents

Introduction

Congratulations on purchasing *Stock Trading for Beginners* and thank you for doing so.

The following chapters will discuss the basic procedures for stock trading so that you can be an expert as soon as possible and begin profiting off different types of stock trading.

With plenty of books with that talks about the subject, are so happy to share this work as we made each and every step to make sure information is useful and enjoyable as needed! We appreciate you chose this book and have a great read!

Chapter 1: Bull and bear periods in the history of Wall Street

The stock market rally that commenced over nine years back during the money related emergency is currently apparently the longest on record in the United States. The United States stock markets have had a notoriously up and down relationship ever since the initial conceptions. One of the first Presidents to combat the control of the private banks back in the 1800s on the US economy was Andrew Jackson. In fact, his campaign runs on the slogan of getting rid of the bank and he is the only President in history known to have completely paid off the nation's outstanding debt. He managed to kick out the bank's control over the government and the economy of the country, but it lasted only so long. Soon enough, the private banks started getting different charters in different states and they eventually strengthened, particularly after Jackson's time at the White House was up.

Since then, the stock market has been a constant see-saw, experiencing bearish periods and then the inevitable bullish periods. During the late 1800s and early 1900s, several large US corporations had been set up by prominent names such as John D. Rockefeller. The economy was doing just fine until in 190 when there was a catastrophic crash in the economy and a lot of money disappeared. It was a true period of depression as most people were unable to even find fresh food in the streets to eat.

After the crash of the stock market, the Federal Reserve was established in 1912. Since then, the US economy experienced a boom through the 1920s and there were several loans going round. It was a nice period to be living in the United States, people had disposable income, there were several advertisements and the country did not suffer much damage after the First World War. The economy was truly prosperous but a lot of this was to come to an abrupt end in 1929 when the economy of the United States experienced another crash.

The market in the United States has been experiencing different levels of bearish and bullish trends. However, the economy has rapidly grown and is the largest in the world. The Chinese economy follows, however it will take a lot for the United States to cede the infamous title of having the largest economy. It is a title they have held for a long time and the economy continues to expand with different financial measures and policies being undertaken. Historically, despite the size of the economy, the bullish and bearish trends are numerous.

One of the most infamous periods in the economy of the nation was the crash of the stock market and subsequent financial systems in 2008. The news was greeted with shock all over the world and it ended up rapidly affecting the standards of living in various countries. The price of oil was also quite inconsistent, at some point shooting up to record levels and sometimes sinking below expectations. The crashing of the US economy was a monumental event that ended up affecting other stock markets around the world. The stability of the US economy makes it easier to trade stocks and invest in different markets.

There are a number of lessons that one can learn from the history of the United States economy to implement to success. First, it is possible to experience bullish and bearish trends on an investment that you were willing to put only a single trend. It is important to spread your risk when you have large stakes because it provides a slight surety that your money will come. However, it is still possible to make a loss and this should be used as a learning point for future trades.

Another important lesson that can be learned from the upheaval nature of the US economy is that it is necessary to follow trends carefully. Those who managed to put money on the eventual demise of the housing market in 2008 as early as 2002 ended up profiting big-time. It is necessary to closely follow the important aspects of an economy when trading stocks. This gives you the first-hand information you require to follow up on specific investments in order to profit from them. Despite many people taking out loans and making specific trends look popular, only those who spent their time researching the current state of affairs came out slightly dented from the economic crash.

Wall Street has represented a pivotal role in the economy of the United States. The crash of the economy in 2008 had all eyes looking in that direction, but most of the directors and heads of banks were paid hefty commissions. What happens in Wall Street should be basic information for anybody looking to trade in the stock market. Understand the workings of the system and do not get bored by all the jargon that you will encounter. Instead, use this as a learning opportunity to enhance your knowledge of trading so that you can achieve success.

From the history of the United States economy, it is also possible to get the lesson on patience. The economy has increasingly grown as a result of patient strategies that have worked during both wartime and peacetime. The country's economy has slowly been expanding, rapidly changing standards of living through the decade. Other large countries in Europe such as Germany and the United Kingdom have taken a longer period of time to expand as compared to the United States. The level of capital available to the US is tremendous and enables the economy to grow much rapidly than other nations. As a stock trader, it is necessary to remain alert to all opportunities because you never know the next big thing. However, this requires a lot of patience and commitment because one high-risk strategy that works will yield tremendous benefit.

Everyone discusses bull and bear markets, particularly the present one regularly called the longest bull showcase in history at just shy of 3,800 days. Be that as it may, no one appears to concede to an accurate definition, or knows where the overarching ones started, including numerous investment experts.

Investigators regularly state that a bull market is characterized by a 20% ascent from a market file's latest absolute bottom; a bear advertises, a 20% decrease from its most recent high.

Minor departure from that is innumerable—and perpetually confounding. Just by glancing back at the historical backdrop of these terms would you be able to can show signs of improvement feeling of what they mean, why they matter and how you should figure them your reasoning.

The utilization of "bull" and "bear" to allude to monetary positive thinkers and worrywarts, separately, started in Britain in the mid-eighteenth century.

"Bull" evoked the howling of an enthusiastic purchaser. "Bear" seems to have originated from an early world-renowned articulation, "to sell the bear's skin before one has gotten the bear"— a well-suited allegory for a short deal, in which a trader sells acquired offers in order to buy them back at a lower cost.

The expressions "bull market" and "bear showcase," in any case, did not emerge until the 1850s. And still, after all that, they frequently alluded to just a solitary day's activity.

As late as 1874, when Matthew Hale Smith distributed his annual "Bulls and Bears of New York," the expression "bull showcase" still looked peculiar to perusers. "They never purchase on what is known as a Bull showcase," Smith expounded on driving theorists, "yet consistently when stocks are low."

For a considerable length of time, bull and bear markets alluded not too long haul moves in the stock market in general, however to transient value activity in a solitary resource.

"The bull showcase in wheat Saturday kept going about 60 minutes," announced The Wall Street Journal on May 15, 1899.

The absolute first issue of the Journal, on July 8, 1889, announced: "The bull market of 1885 started July 2," with the normal cost of 12 stocks (counting Pacific Mail Steamship and Western Union) at 61.49, and topped May 18, 1887, at 93.27. That was almost a 52% addition.

Be that as it may, the Journal did not characterize a bull advertise, and numerous decades would go before it did.

Charles Henry Dow, fellow benefactor of the Journal, composed—not in all respects accommodatingly—in 1902: "It is a bull period as long as the normal of one high point surpasses that of past high focuses. It is a bear period when the depressed spot moves toward becoming lower than the past depressed spots."

Notwithstanding during the thundering 1920s, the Journal once in a while utilized the expression "bull advertise."

In December 1949, the Magazine of Wall Street stated: "It is essentially unrealistic to land at an exact meaning of so factor a thing as a bull market or bear advertise." Settling on "an extensive ascent in stock costs over a significant timeframe," the magazine referred to the activity in the Dow between May 1947 and June 1948—an 18% increase—for instance of a bull showcase.

The 20% limit for bull and bear markets started to grab hold just "in the last 1950s and mid-1960s. It turned into the seed around which accord framed, helped mostly by the money related press including Dow Jones, the Journal's parent embracing it as a shortsighted—and brief—definition.

An article in the New York Times on July 23, 1962, pegged May 28 of that year as the start of a bear market. That was the day the S&P 500 was first down 20% from its high in 1961. The 20% edge set aside a long effort to pick up footing, be that as it may.

In January 1967, as the Dow moved toward a 14% addition from its trough the past October, the Journal said numerous experts were at that point "articulating the words 'bull market' again without precedent for an extended period of time."

On Sept. 13, 1970, with stocks as of now up 22% off their lows that spring, the Times still idea it was too early to pronounce a bull market.

Simply after the epic execution of the 1980s and 1990s, when stocks conveyed generally 18% normal yearly returns, did the definitions with a 20% limit grab hold for good.

Where does this leave financial specialists?

In the first place, acknowledge how subjective the expressions "bull market" and "bear market" are. Nobody knows why the definitions do exclude a base period of time. Or on the other hand for what reason they're typically founded on shutting costs rather than intraday highs and lows. Or then again who concocted the 20% limit and why it wasn't 25% or 30% or 41.2879%. (Characterizing a "redress" as a 10% decrease is similarly discretionary.)

Consider that the terms can make an unavoidable outcome. From Sept. 20 through Dec. 24, 2018, the S&P 500 declined 19.78% dependent on shutting costs, barely missing the regular meaning of a bear market. Utilizing intraday evaluating, the S&P declined 20.21% from Sept. 21 through Dec. 26.

Had stocks shut an unimportant 0.22% lower last Christmas Eve, features—incorporating into the Journal—would have perused something like stocks enters bear-market an area.

A lot more speculators and money related consultants may have sold stocks accordingly, apparently extending the decay.

Rather, the 19.78% tumble empowered the market to delay without freezing and, at last, to continue its ascent in 2019.

Financial specialists consistently need more accuracy than the aggregate emotional episodes of markets will in general offer. For this situation, the way that the decay was barely short of 20% seems to have given financial specialists the certainty that the market hadn't entered bear an area—and changed their conduct.

The more you think about money related history, the less astounded you ought to be by how bull and bear markets unfurl.

Chapter 2: Exchange Traded Funds

ETFs are a sort of exchange traded investment item that must enroll with the SEC under the 1940 Act as either an open-end investment organization (for the most part known as "reserves") or a unit investment trust.

The graph below shows the growth of ETF through the decades;

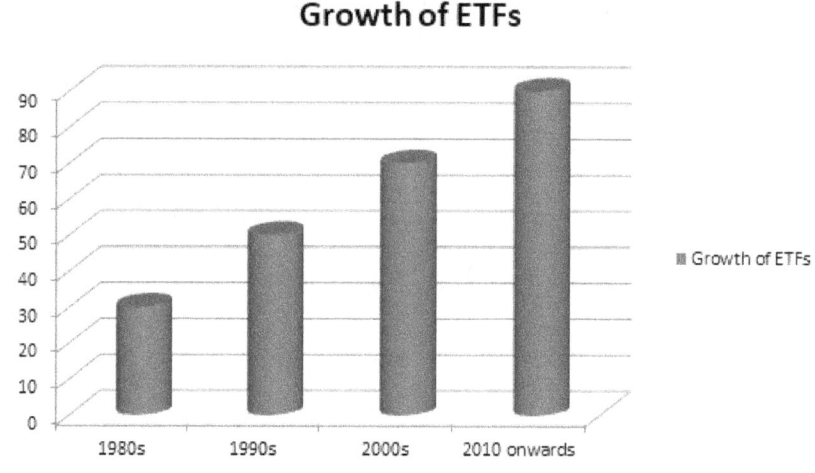

Growth of ETFs

Like common assets, ETFs offer speculators an approach to pooling their cash in a reserve that makes investments in stocks, bonds, or different resources and, consequently, to get enthusiasm for that investment pool. In contrast to common assets, nonetheless, ETF offers are traded on a national stock trade and at market costs that could possibly be equivalent to the net resource esteem ("NAV") of the offers, that is, the estimation of the ETF's advantages less its liabilities partitioned by the number of offers extraordinary.

ETFs are not shared assets. For the most part, ETFs join highlights of a common reserve, which can be obtained or reclaimed toward the part of the arrangement day at its NAV per share, with the intraday trading highlight of a shut end support, whose offers trade all through the trading day at market costs.

Not at all like with common reserve shares, retail financial specialists can just buy and sell ETF partake in market exchanges. That is, not normal for common assets, ETFs do not sell individual offers legitimately to, or recover their individual offers straightforwardly from, retail speculators. Rather, ETF supporters go into legally binding associations with at least one financial establishments known as "Approved Participants." Authorized Participants normally are enormous specialist vendors. Just Authorized Participants are allowed to buy and reclaim shares straightforwardly from the ETF, and they can do as such just in enormous collections or squares (e.g., 50,000 ETF shares) normally called "Creation Units."

Different financial specialists buy and sell ETF partakes in market exchanges at market costs. An ETF's market value ordinarily will be pretty much than the store's NAV per share. This is on the grounds that the ETF's market cost vacillates during the trading day because of an assortment of components, including the fundamental costs of the ETF's advantages and the interest for the ETF, while the ETF's NAV is the estimation of the ETF's benefits short its liabilities, as determined by the ETF toward the part of the bargain day.

Sorts of ETFs

Record Based ETFs

Most ETFs trading in the marketplace is record based ETFs. These ETFs look to follow a securities list like the S&P 500 stock record and for the most part, but fundamentally in the segment securities of the file. For instance, the SPDR, or "insect" ETF, which looks to follow the S&P 500 stock file, puts resources into most of the majority of the value securities contained in the S&P 500 stock list. A few, however not all, ETFs may post their property on their sites every day.

Effectively Managed ETFs

Effectively oversaw ETFs are not founded on a list. Rather, they try to accomplish an expressed investment objective by putting resources into an arrangement of stocks, bonds, and different resources. Dissimilar to with a record based ETF, a guide of an effectively overseen ETF may effectively purchase or sell parts in the portfolio once a day regardless of congruity with a file.

Prior to putting resources into an ETF, you should peruse the two its synopsis plan and its full outline, which give definite data on the ETF's investment objective, head investment systems, risks, costs, and recorded execution (if any). The SEC's EDGAR framework, just as Internet web crawlers, can enable you to find a specific ETF plan. You can likewise discover plans on the sites of the financial firms that support a specific ETF, just as through your agent.

Try not to put resources into something that you do not get it. If you can't clarify the investment opportunity in a couple of words and in a justifiable manner, you may need to rethink the potential investment.

At last, you may wish to think about looking for the exhortation of an investment proficient. If you do, make sure to work with somebody who comprehends your investment goals and resistance for risk. Your investment expert ought to comprehend complex items and have the option to disclose agreeable to you whether or how they fit with your goals.

Trade-traded reserves (ETFs) are securities that intently look like file reserves, however, can be purchased and sold during the day simply like regular stocks. These investment vehicles permit financial specialists a helpful method to buy a wide bin of securities in a solitary exchange. Basically, ETFs offer the accommodation of stock alongside the diversification of a shared reserve.

Trade-traded assets are the absolute most well known and inventive new securities to hit the market since the presentation of the shared store. The principal ETF was the Standard and Poor's Deposit Receipt (SPDR, or "Insect"), which was first propelled in 1993. Obtaining Spiders gave financial specialists an approach to copy the exhibition of the S&P 500 without acquiring list support. Moreover, on the grounds that they traded like a stock, SPDRs could be purchased and sold for the duration of the day, bought on edge, or even undercuts.

At whatever point a speculator buys an ETF, the person in question is essentially putting resources into the presentation of a fundamental heap of securities - for the most part, those speaking to a specific list or division. Unit Investment Trusts (UITs) are regularly sorted out in a similar way. Be that as it may, the unordinary legitimate structure of an ETF makes the item fairly interesting.

Trade-traded assets do not sell shares straightforwardly to speculators. Rather, every ETF's support issues huge squares (regularly of 50,000 offers or more) that are known as creation units. These units are then purchased by an "approved member" - commonly a market producer, expert or institutional financial specialist - which gets portions of the basic securities and spots them in a trust. The approved member at that point separates these creation units into ETF shares - every one of which speaks to a legitimate case to a little part of the benefits in the creation unit - and after that sells them on an auxiliary market.

Similarly, as shut end assets do not generally trade at a value that accurately mirrors the estimation of the fundamental resources in each portion of the portfolio, it is likewise workable for an ETF to trade at a higher cost than normal or a markdown to its genuine worth. To exchange their possessions, most financial specialists basically sell their ETF offers to different speculators on the open market. In any case, it is conceivable to accumulate enough ETF offers to recover them for one creation unit and after that reclaim the creation unit for the basic securities. In view of the huge number of offers included, singular financial specialists only from time to time utilize this alternative.

Trade-traded assets have become progressively prevalent as of late, and the quantity of contributions has swelled. Today, these securities contend with shared assets and offer various points of interest over their antecedents, including:

Minimal effort - Unlike customary common and record reserves, ETFs have no front-or back-end loads. Furthermore, on the grounds that they are not effectively overseen, most ETFs have insignificant cost proportions, making them substantially more moderate than most other diversified investment vehicles. Most common assets likewise have the least investment necessities, making them unreasonable for some littler financial specialists. On the other hand, financial specialists can buy as meager as one portion of their preferred ETF.

Liquidity - Whereas customarily shared assets are just estimated toward the day's end, ETFs can be purchased and sold whenever all through the trading day. Many have normal everyday trading volumes in the several thousand (and now and again millions) of offers every day, making them amazingly fluid.

Expense Advantages - In a customary shared reserve, directors are normally compelled to auction portfolio resources so as to meet reclamations. Frequently, this demonstration triggers capital increases charges, to which all investors are uncovered. On the other hand, the purchasing and selling of offers on the open market has no effect on an ETF's assessment obligation, and those that recover their ETFs are paid in portions of stock as opposed to in real money. This limits an ETF's taxation rate since it does not need to sell shares (and in this manner possibly acknowledge assessable capital additions) to acquire money to come back to financial specialists. Moreover, the individuals who reclaim their ETFs are paid with the least cost-premise partakes in the reserve, which builds the cost reason for the rest of the property, consequently limiting the ETF's capital increases introduction.

Despite the fact that trade traded assets offer a few favorable circumstances over conventional shared assets, they likewise have two unmistakable weaknesses. To start, the securities that an ETF tracks are, to a great extent fixed. Therefore, financial specialists that favor dynamic administration will most likely discover ETFs completely inadmissible. Moreover, in light of the fact that they trade like stocks, every ETF buy will be charged a financier commission. For those that make normal occasional investments - for example, a month to month dollar-cost averaging investment plan - these common commissions may rapidly progress toward becoming cost-restrictive.

Similarly, as with any security, the upsides and downsides ought to be gauged cautiously, and financial specialists should initially get their work done to decide if trade traded assets are the proper vehicle to meet their individual objectives and targets.

Chapter 3: About Brokers and Fees

To purchase and sell stocks, securities, and shared assets, you need a dealer. A representative can either be an individual authorized operator or a business firm like Merrill Lynch, Smith Barney or Charles Schwab. The most fundamental capacity of an agent is to execute trades for the financial specialist, yet numerous intermediaries offer extra administrations like investment exhortation and the portfolio of the executives. Representatives make cash by charging commissions on each trade and gathering expenses from financial specialists.

It is critical to see how these commissions and expenses work. Above all else, most specialists require a base store in your investment fund. It is like a financial balance, and the dealer will pull back cash from it each time the person needs to make a trade. The normal least store is somewhere in the range of $500 and $2,500, yet it is normal for essentials to be as high as $10,000. If you can't supply the base store, you can't work with the dealer, so search for that data first.

As we referenced, dealers make cash by charging a commission on each trade. The sum a dealer charge shifts enormously among markdown and full-administration merchants. Generally, rebate specialists do not do anything besides execute the trade. Numerous online specialists, along these lines, are markdown intermediaries. You round out the subtleties of the trade on the Web website, hit "purchase" or "sell" and somebody on the opposite end makes the exchange. Markdown specialists can charge as meager as $5 to $15 per trade.

Full-administration representatives do significantly more than simply execute trades. They're proficient cash directors and financial organizers who work with a customer to build up a reasonable investment technique and keep up a portfolio that supports that system. Since full-administration dealers do impressive market research and meet face to face with every customer, the normal full-administration commission is somewhere in the range of $100 and $200 a trade.

Notwithstanding commissions, dealers likewise charge yearly support and working expenses. A few intermediaries even charge latency expenses if you go for a considerable length of time without making a trade. What's more, others charge least equalization expenses if your investment fund plunges underneath a specific level or sum. Prior to working with a merchant, ensure you comprehend what charges apply to your record and how they will be determined.

As a starting financial specialist, it very well may be difficult to pick between a rebate and full-administration intermediary. Markdown representatives are shabby, yet you get what you pay for: A rebate agent does not get paid to offer you guidance. Then again, not all full-administration intermediaries merit their heavy payments. Some are seemingly sales reps who just sell their business association's investment items. As we talked about before, they get paid by the trade. Some full-administration intermediaries have been blamed for urging customers to make various, pointless trades which are an untrustworthy practice called agitating.

Fortunately, there is another age of online expedites that fall someplace in the rebate and full-administration limits. You will pay somewhere in the range of $15 and $30 per trade, however, you will get more direction and backing than from a customary rebate dealer. Also, presently some full-administration agents are offering limited, online-just trades. When you have an expedite, it is an ideal opportunity to build up an investment procedure.

There are two different sorts of business firms: full administration and markdown. The differences between the two and the expenses they charge are significant. Here's a short manual for how financier charges work with the two kinds of firms.

What Are Brokerage Fees?

When all is said in done, financier expenses are charges the merchant charges you to hold and deal with your investments. These charges may incorporate yearly expenses, expenses for investigating investment information, and dormancy expenses if you are not trading consistently. It is significant you know about the different sorts of business charges, just as the kinds of agents accessible to deal with your investments.

Full-Service Broker

Full-administration merchants are paid commissions dependent on exchanges. The normal charge per exchange at a full-administration dealer is $150. This is much lower than in the past yet at the same time a lot higher than rebate agents where by and large exchange costs around $10.

At a full-administration intermediary, you are paying a premium for research, training, and guidance. In any case, recall that full-administration intermediaries are likewise sales reps.

There are additionally some full-administration expedites that charge a yearly expense somewhere in the range of 1% and 1.5% of absolute resources oversaw for a customer who does not charge per trade. If you do not feel great looking into and making your very own trades, this is a decent alternative to consider. These agents will likewise have a motivation to perform well in such a case that your portfolio performs resources under administration increment, which means they make more for overseeing them.

Markdown Broker

Markdown merchants by and large do not offer investment counsel. Trading charges for online rebate agents run somewhere in the range of $4.95 to $20, however, most are somewhere in the range of $7 and $10. This rate is liable to change since markdown agents are reliably bringing down their charges so as to draw in more clients and increase market share. Some even offer free trades. If you get, your work is done limit dealers can spare you a ton of cash with regards to exchange costs.

Doing Your Own Research

Most financial specialists try not to peruse Securities and Exchange Commission (SEC) filings, yet SEC filings are accessible to general society and the data inside them resembles taking an open book test. The appropriate responses are accommodated you. Not at all like official statements, must an open organization express the certainties in its SEC filings. This makes it generally simple to research stocks.

Additionally, give close consideration to industry patterns. If quick easygoing evolved ways of life that offer common and natural sustenance are in, go with the pattern, not against it. Do your exploration to decide the best of the breed. Also, you do not have to plunge that profound. When in doubt, if the more extensive market is hot, income development will be the key factor driving stock value appreciation. Financial specialists and traders love income development in bull market conditions. If the more extensive market is cool, net gain development and a solid asset report will be the keys to progress. Speculators and traders like to race to the well-being for profits and offer buybacks in these conditions.

If you are rash as well as not willing to get your work done, at that point you ought to consider a full-administration dealer. Something else, a markdown intermediary, which enables you to execute trades, however, does not offer investment guidance, is a superior choice.

Chapter 4: Platforms for Investing in Stocks

In the development of portable selection in the online monetary space, exchange your money market fund from an online stage still has a lot of advantages. A portion of these advantages incorporates an extensive assortment of request kinds for alternatives merchants, exhaustive graphing apparatuses for informal investors, the capacity to make security stepping stools, and instructive encounters that aid creates you increasingly arranged to contribute and trade. The victors in this classification had great web-based trading entryways that furnish you with a plenitude of highlights to enable you to accomplish.

Charles Schwab

Schwab clients can exploit their ETF OneSource rundown, which presents more than 200 without commission exchange-traded assets from 16 diverse store families. The ETF screener on the site has 9 pre-characterized screens, or you can develop your own with to 70 diverse benchmarks, consist of execution, division, risk measures, and portfolio substance.

There are three electronic destinations accessible: the standard at schwab.com, in addition to Trade Source, which enables clients to create trading thoughts, and Street Smart Central, which incorporates propelled alternatives examination and a live news source from CNBC. Trade Source's Strategy Screener gives you a chance to pick plain English screens, for example, "Which stocks have been up to or down on a higher than typical level of the market's absolute volume?" A high-tech examination from Recognia energizes the screener.

Charles Schwab additionally got honors for Best Overall Online Brokers, Best for International Trading, Best for Options Trading, Best for Penny Stocks, Best for Beginners, Best for Roth IRAs, Best for IRAs, Best for ETFs, and Best Stock Trading Apps.

Masters

Alternatives traders can utilize the intense liability examination worked by optionsXpress, a financier Schwab obtained and incorporated into their StreetSmart Edge site

The All-in-One Trade Ticket gives you a chance to construct a transaction for any advantage types you are qualified to use, along with alternatives, prospects, and fates choices

The Idea Hub gives you a chance to search for trading thoughts dependent on market moves, up and coming income declarations, premium gathering and secured calls, in addition to prospects choices. You can select trading thought, run examination, and afterward hit the Trade catch and open a position.

Cons

There are three web stages, and you may wind up exchanging amidst them to utilize every one of the instruments you need

The outlining usefulness in StreetSmart Central keeps running on Adobe Flash, which explains issues with some working frameworks

TD Ameritrade

Gushing news and home-developed video is worked into the TD Ameritrade site, alongside an abundance of instruction and item contributions. You can peruse the prattle about your property and watch records utilizing Social Signals, which pulls data from Twitter and composes tweets for you. You can alter your web experience utilizing TD Ameritrade's Dock instrument, which gives you a chance to incorporate data from different sites, for example, Yahoo! Money.

TD Ameritrade likewise got honors for Best Overall Online Brokers, Best for Day Trading, Best for Options Trading, Best for Beginners, Best for ETFs, Best for Roth IRAs, Best for IRAs and Best Stock Trading Apps.

Professionals

Effectively characterized cautions let you characterize what sorts of reports you need, and how every now and again you need them conveyed

Free autonomous exploration from an immense assortment of origins
An exchange ticket is shown at the base of each screen, so you can make a brisk move on your thoughts

A watch shows you set up on your web stage will likewise show on a versatile application

Gains Keeper, a capital additions screen, is allowed to utilize

Cons

Higher than normal compensations and edge rates

An overabundance of highlights over various stages can make it elusive the apparatuses you need

Complex choices (multiple legs) can't be traded on the web stage

Fates and forex can't be traded on the web stage

E*TRADE

E*TRADE's standard web stage incorporates spilling continuous statements, news, graphs, and day by day market critique. You will discover screeners to enable you to pick stocks, ETFs, shared assets, and bonds depending on your benchmark. Those unfamiliar to contributing can assemble redid procedures to study choosing and putting trades, and furthermore go to online classes and live occasions to venture up to increasingly complex procedures.

Choices traders can utilize screeners and streamlining agents worked by expert market producers on the OptionsHouse stage. You can close a value choice evaluated at $0.10 or less for nothing with the Dime Buyback Program. Propelled traders can examine and trade alternatives on prospects nonstop.

E*TRADE likewise got honors for Best for Options Trading, Best for ETFs, Best Stock Trading Apps, Best for Roth IRAs, Best for IRAs, and Best for Beginners.

Professionals

The OptionsHouse stage incorporates recordings and adding machines to enable you to figure out how – and why – to trade alternatives.

The Technical Insights highlight on the OptionsHouse stage shows the new specialized examiner how to utilize these examinations.

Beyond what 250 ETFs can be traded without commission.

You can get your portfolio fully operational rapidly with one of E*TRADE's prebuilt ETF portfolios, all of which use sans commission reserves. (Least $2,500).

Great apparatuses and level evaluating for bond traders ($1 per bond).

Cons

Commissions and edge rates are on the high side except if you are a regular trader

You may need to switch forward and backward between the E*TRADE site and the OptionsHouse stage to exploit all the accessible devices
No forex or global trading accessible

Merrill Edge

Merrill's site offers a great deal of assistance for defining and achieving financial objectives. The Personal Retirement Calculator causes you to gauge the amount you will have to resign, and after that fabricates an activity intend to help with increasing your riches. The Portfolio Story highlight illuminates how your benefits are designated by part and class, and causes you to define failing to meet expectations investments to produce higher returns.

The exploration highlights outline investigators' assessments of your possessions. You can likewise look at the Environmental, Social and Governance (ESG) scores to perceive how your investments line up with your own qualities. The propelled web stage, Merrill Edge MarketPro, highlights spilling statements and news alongside intelligent diagramming. The MarketPro dashboard is adaptable, enabling you to revamp the apparatuses to suit your needs.

Merrill Edge additionally got honors for Best for Beginners, Best Stock Trading Apps, Best for IRAs, and Best for Roth IRAs.

Experts

Bunches of assistance for getting ready for objectives and surveying your advancement

Life stage arranging gives you specific direction for your present circumstance: simply beginning, building riches, nearing retirement, and living in retirement

Widely coordinated with parent Bank of America

Those with high adjusts with Merrill and additionally, Bank of America can qualify for sans commission stock and ETF trading

Cons

MarketPro access requires either a high parity or successive trading action

Successive pushing to move resources into an oversaw record, which can cost more

No without commission ETFs accessible, however, clients with high adjust with Merrill and additionally Bank of America can qualify for 30-100 free stock/ETF trades a month to month

The deferred commissions for premium individuals can't be utilized for alternatives trades

Constancy Investments

Constancy highlights outstanding amongst other trade-steering motors, which produced in diminished exchange costs for their clients. The objective of their trading innovation is to accomplish value enhancement for client orders, so that "Purchase" orders are carried out at a value lower than the market right now the trade is put, and "Sell" orders complete at a more expensive rate. Clients trading amounts more than 500 offers can regularly accomplish more value on upgrade than they pay in commission. Constancy's portfolio investigation highlight gives you a chance to connect outside records, just as any cryptographic money you hold at Coinbase, to provide you an image of your, generally speaking, financial wellbeing.

Instruction contributions and expense arranging are well incorporated, and the site itself is easy to explore. They are as of late upgraded exchange ticket lessens the number of snaps expected to put a trade. Constancy suggests an increasingly intricate exchange site called Trade Armor for the individuals who need to structure a leave plan when opening another position.

The site highlights screeners for stocks, exchange-traded reserves (ETFs), common assets, and an assortment of fixed pay items.

Loyalty likewise got honors for Best Overall Online Brokers, Best for Beginners, Best Stock Trading Apps, and Best for ETFs, Best for Penny Stocks, Best for Roth IRAs, Best for IRAs and Best for International Trading.

Aces

Low commissions tied with phenomenal training and research

Screeners incorporate social duty, and subjects, for example, 3-D printing, artificial insight, organizer run firms, and the sky is the limit from there

Banking administrations pitches, incorporate a 2% money back Visa and ATM charge discounts

For choices traders, a trade ticket has been incorporated into the choices chain see

Portfolio investigation enables clients to comprehend their presentation to divisions, ventures, and geological areas

Cons

The site performed inconsistently during trading floods in the most recent year

No fates trading accessible

The visitor gets to accessible for 30 days; must store assets to keep up access to explore, cites, and so forth.

A few highlights are elusive because of the profound menu structure of the site.

Chapter 5: How to Read Charts

If you are going to effectively trade stocks as a stock market financial specialist, at that point you have to realize how to peruse stock charts. Indeed, even traders who essentially utilize major investigation to choose stocks to put resources into still frequently utilize specialized examination of stock value development to decide specific purchase or passage, and sell, or leave, focuses.

Stock charts are unreservedly accessible on sites, for example, Google Finance and Yahoo Finance, and stock financiers consistently make stock charts accessible for their customers. To put it plainly, you shouldn't experience any difficulty discovering stock charts to inspect.

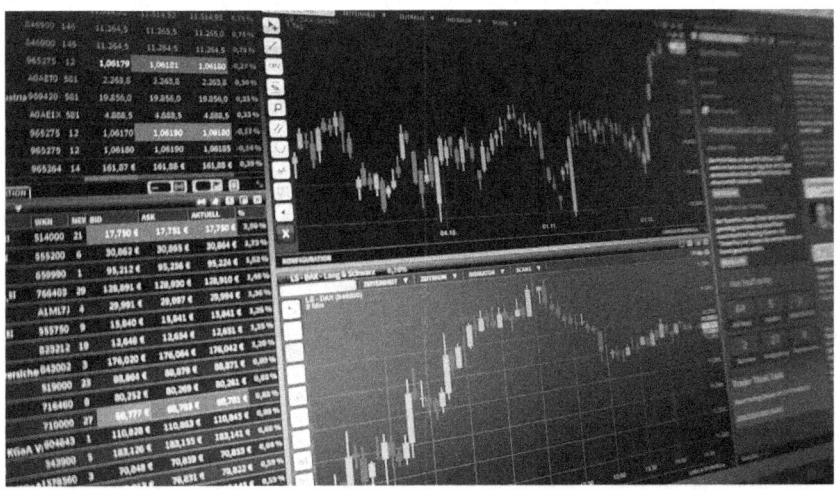

Stock Chart Construction – Lines, Bars, Candlesticks

Stock charts can fluctuate in their development from bar charts to candle charts to line charts to point and figure charts. About every single stock chart give you the alternative to switch between the different sorts of charts, just as the capacity to overlay different specialized pointers on a chart. You can likewise differ the time period appeared by a chart. While everyday charts are likely the most usually utilized, intraday, week by week, month to month, year-to-date (YTD), 5-year, 10-year, and a total verifiable lifetime of stock are additionally accessible.

There are relative preferences and weaknesses in utilizing different chart development styles and utilizing different time periods for examination. What style and time period will work best for you as an individual investigator or speculator is something that you can just find through really doing stock chart examination. You can gather significant signs of plausible stock value development from any stock chart. You ought to pick the chart style that makes it least demanding for you to peruse and break down the chart, and trade beneficially.

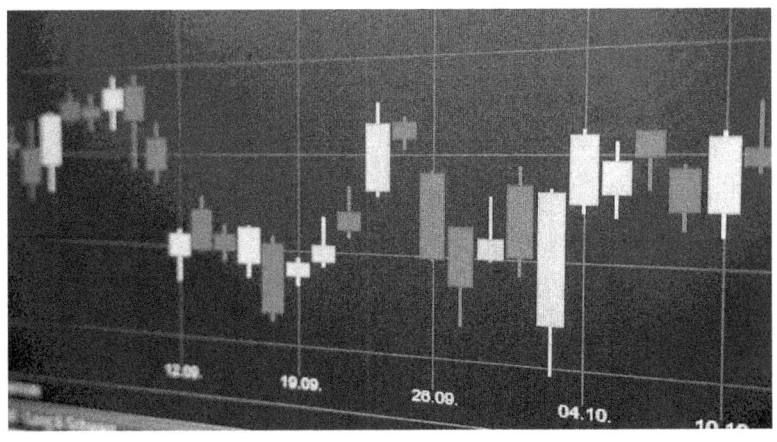

Taking a gander at a Stock Chart

The following is a year-to-date every day chart of Apple Inc. (AAPL), politeness of stockcharts.com. This chart is a candle chart, with white candles showing up days for the stock and red candles appearing down days. Also, this chart has a few specialized pointers included: a 50-period moving normal and a 200-period moving normal, showing up as blue and red lines on the chart; the relative quality marker (RSI) which shows up in a different window over the primary chart window; the moving normal union disparity pointer (MACD) which shows up in a different window underneath the chart.

Along the base of the fundamental chart window, the everyday trading volume appears. Note the huge spike in volume that happened on February first, when the stock gapped higher and started a solid upswing which went on until early June. Likewise, note the high measure of selling volume (shown by red volume bars which demonstrate days with a more prominent measure of selling volume than purchasing volume) that happens when the stock moves forcefully descending around June twelfth.

Volume in Stock Chart Analysis

The volume shows up on almost every stock chart that you will discover. That is on the grounds that trading volume is viewed as a basic specialized marker by about each stock financial specialist. On the chart above, notwithstanding demonstrating all out-degree of trading volume for every day, days with more prominent purchasing volume are shown with blue bars and days with more noteworthy selling volume are shown with red bars.

The reason that volume is viewed as a significant specialized marker is a basic one. By far most of stock market purchasing and selling is finished by enormous institutional traders, for example, investment banks, and by store chiefs, for example, common reserve or exchange-traded subsidize (ETF) directors. At the point when those financial specialists make significant buys or offers of stock, it makes high trading volume, and it is that sort of real purchasing and selling by huge speculators that ordinarily move a stock higher or lower.

In this manner, individual or other institutional traders watch volume figures for signs of real purchasing or selling action by huge establishments. This data can be utilized either to conjecture a future value pattern for the stock or to identify key value backing and obstruction levels.

Indeed, numerous individual financial specialists decide their purchasing and selling choices exclusively dependent on following the identified activities of major institutional traders. They purchase stocks when volume and value development demonstrate that real establishments are purchasing, and sell or abstain from purchasing stocks when there indicate major institutional selling.

Such a methodology works best when connected to real stocks that are commonly intensely traded. It will probably be less viable when connected to stocks of little organizations that are not yet on the radar screens of enormous institutional financial specialists and that have generally little trading volumes even on days when the stock is more intensely traded than expected.

Essential Volume Patterns

There are four essential volume designs that traders normally watch as markers.

High volume trading on Up Days – This is a bullish sign that a stock's cost will keep on rising

Low volume trading on Down Days – This is additionally a bullish sign since it demonstrates that on days when the stock's value falls back a piece, relatively few speculators are associated with the trading. In this manner, such down days happening in a general bull market are ordinarily deciphered as transitory retracements or remedies as opposed to as pointers of future significant value development.

High Volume Trading on Down Days – This is viewed as a bearish pointer for a stock, as it demonstrates that major institutional traders are forcefully selling the stock.

Low Volume Trading on Up Days – This is another bearish marker, despite the fact that not as solid as high volume trading on down days. The low volume will, in general, peg the trading activity on such days as less significant and for the most part proof of only a transient counter-pattern retracement upward in an in general, long haul bearish pattern.

Utilizing Technical Indicators

In examining stock charts for stock market contributing, financial specialists utilize an assortment of specialized pointers to help them all the more correctly likely value development, to identify patterns, and to envision market inversions from bullish patterns to bearish patterns and the other way around.

One of the most generally utilized specialized markers is moving normally. The moving midpoints that are most every now and again connected to day by day stock charts are the 20-day, 50-day, and 200-day moving normally. For the most part talking, up to a shorter period moving normal is over a more drawn out period moving normal, a stock is viewed as in a general upturn. On the other hand, if shorter-term moving midpoints are beneath longer-term moving midpoints, at that point that demonstrates a general downtrend.

The Importance of the 200-Day Moving Average

The 200-day moving normal is considered by most examiners as a basic marker on a stock chart. Traders who are bullish on a stock need to see the stock's cost stay over the 200-day moving normally. Bearish traders who are undercutting a stock need to see the stock value remain underneath the 200-day moving normally. If a stock's value crosses from beneath the 200-day moving normal to above it, this is typically deciphered as a bullish market inversion. A drawback cross of cost from over the 200-day moving normal is deciphered as a bearish sign for the stock.

The exchange between the 50-day and 200-day moving midpoints is likewise considered as a solid marker for future value development. At the point when the 50-day moving normal crosses from beneath to over the 200-day moving normal, this occasion is alluded to by specialized investigators as a "brilliant cross". A brilliant cross is fundamentally a sign that the stock is "gold", set at generously greater expenses.

On the other side, if the 50-day moving normal crosses from above to beneath the 200-day moving normal, this is alluded to by examiners as a "demise cross". You can likely make sense of alone that a "demise cross" isn't considered to look good at a stock's future cost development.

Pattern and Momentum Indicators

There is for all intents and purposes a perpetual rundown of specialized markers for traders to browse in investigating a chart. Investigation with different markers to find the ones that work best for your specific style of trading, and as connected to the specific stocks that you trade. You will likely locate that a few pointers work very well for you in estimating value development for certain stocks however for nobody else.

Specialized investigators regularly use markers of different kinds related to one another. Specialized markers are classified into two essential sorts: pattern pointers, for example, moving midpoints, and force pointers, for example, the MACD or the normal directional record (ADX). Pattern pointers are utilized to identify the general bearing of a stock's cost, up or down, while force markers measure the quality of value development.

Investigating Trends

When evaluating a stock chart, notwithstanding deciding the stock's general pattern, up or down, it is additionally useful to hope to identify parts of a pattern, for example, the accompanying:

To what extent has a pattern been set up? Stocks do not remain in upturns or downtrends uncertainly. In the end, there are consistently pattern changes. If a pattern has proceeded for an extensive stretch of time with no significant restorative retracement moves the other way, you need to be particularly alert for indications of a looming market inversion.

How does a stock will in general trade? A few stocks move in generally moderate, well-characterized patterns. Different stocks will in general experience greater instability all the time, with value making sharp go up or down even amidst a general long haul pattern. If you are trading a stock that regularly proves high instability, at that point you know not to put an excess of significance on the trading activity in any single day.

Are there indications of a conceivable pattern inversion? Cautious examination of stock value development regularly uncovers indications of potential pattern inversions. Force pointers frequently demonstrate a pattern coming up short on steam before the cost of stock really tops, allowing ready traders the chance to escape a stock at a decent cost before it switches to the drawback. The different candle or other chart examples are likewise frequently used to identify significant market inversions.

Identifying Support and Resistance Levels

Stock charts can be especially useful in identifying backing and obstruction levels for stocks. Bolster levels are value levels where you generally observing crisp purchasing coming in to help a stock's cost and turn it back to the upside. On the other hand, opposition levels speak to costs at which a stock has demonstrated an inclination to flop in endeavoring to move higher, going back to the drawback.

Identifying backing and opposition levels can be particularly useful in trading a stock that will in general trade inside a setup trading range over an extensive stretch of time. Some stock traders, having identified such a stock, will hope to purchase the stock at help levels and sell it at obstruction levels, again and again, getting increasingly more cash as the stock crosses a similar ground on various occasions.

For stocks that have well-identified help and opposition levels, value breakouts past both of those levels can be significant pointers of future value development. For instance, if a stock has recently neglected to break above $50 an offer, yet then at long last do as such, this might be an indication that the stock will move from that point to a significantly more expensive rate level.

The chart of General Electric (GE) beneath demonstrates that the stock traded in a tight extend somewhere in the range of $29 and $30 an offer for a while, yet once the stock cost broke underneath the $29 bolster level, it kept on falling generously lower.

Stock chart investigation isn't reliable, not even in the hands of the most master specialized expert. If it were, each stock financial specialist would be a multi-tycoon. In any case, figuring out how to peruse a stock chart will help turn the chances of being a fruitful stock market financial specialist to support you.

Stock chart examination is an aptitude, and like some other ability, one just turns into a specialist at it through training. Fortunately for all intents and purposes anybody willing to work constantly at breaking down stock charts can move toward becoming, if not a through and through the master, at any rate truly great at it – adequate to improve their general gainfulness in stock market trading. In this manner, it is to your greatest advantage as a financial specialist to start or proceed with your training in stock chart examination.

R: Resistance

S: Support

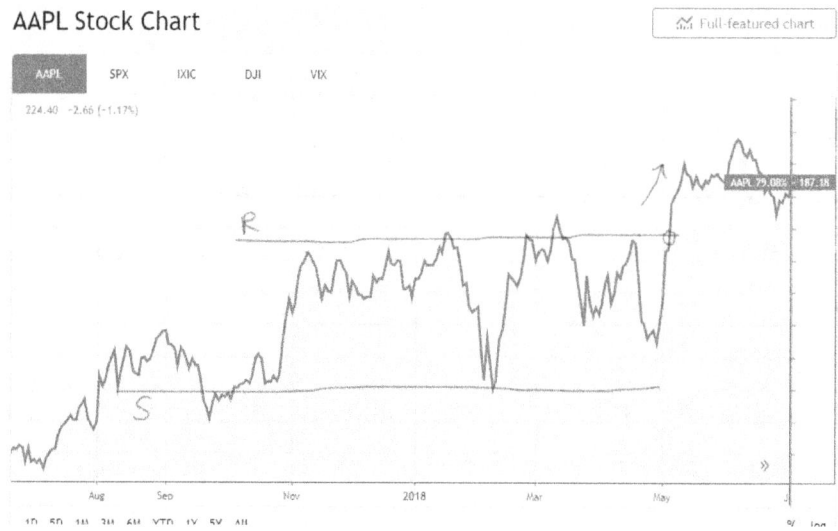

Chapter 6: Bonds, Foreign Stocks, NASDAQ, and Other Assets eg. ETF, IPO

Foreign stocks comprise of different types of assets that can be traded for profit. Stockbrokers usually link customers from around the world to enable them to trade in whatever markets they choose. There are different regulations to consider when trading these assets, such as American-style stocks and European-style stocks. Stockbrokers usually link up their clients into specific markets depending on their demands and their objectives. There are different approaches to trading stocks and it is necessary the first o collect information individually instead of relying on being told what to do every single step.

In order to become a successful trader, you must dedicate a lot of time into the trading practice to enable you to achieve success. This is only possible by understanding the entire process by yourself and spending time with demo accounts to familiarize yourself with the different practices. When you start trading consistently you will realize that foreign stocks have a lot of benefits as compared to the local ones. For one, you can diversify your investments and get into numerous markets, reducing your risks and specializing in trades that you are completely familiar with.

Foreign stocks increase your exposure to the rest of the world and this is extremely important when looking to trade for a living. It is possible to take note of the fact that there are numerous opportunities that keep coming up with foreign stocks, but it will be useful to have a stockbroker because different regulations can limit the scope of your trade.

Investing in foreign stocks has become intensely well-known over the past couple of years and it has enabled more people to start trading actively. They are attractive in several areas because people do not feel limited to single bundles of stock that are only available in their region. Thanks to the internet, it has become possible to trade consistently and regularly in order to make a profit. Now there are numerous people from around the world that are reaping the rewards of foreign stock trading as they can expand their businesses exponentially. There are a lot of opportunities to start new trades and understand new concepts when trading foreign stocks and this is fundamental in ensuring that you become a successful trader.

Optional markets such as NASDAQ and NYSE are stock markets and you will need a broker to successfully make money through this system. The iconic New York Stock Exchange is closely linked to Wall Street and the trading of stocks for profit. You should learn as much as possible about these stock markets in order to get a feel of the different items that are traded and how you can benefit. It is possible for a stockbroker to fill you in on what to expect and the different aspects of trading but only by researching for yourself will you be able to get everything that you need. Read up on the different approaches to trading these stocks as they have become commonplace for those looking for solid investments.

There are different types of loans that are issued for those looking to invest in the stock market. This is the reason why it is important to collect information on the overall methodology o that you are not caught out by surprise. The general process works with you setting up an account and finding a stockbroker to handle your resources. When you take out a loan, the most basic requirement is some form of security, but only do so if you are absolutely ready and well researched. The fact is that most people fail on their first attempt in the stock market and that is why it is better to have capital of your own. Most people take out loans as back-up for capital that already exists and this is a good risk-mitigating strategy as it ensures that there is always capital available to trade.

Factor in different operational costs as well as the fee that the agent will receive a commission for investing your resources. As long as you are in the stock market, you will experience different types of expenses that you simply must be prepared for. You will need a lot of patience if you are going to achieve any success in the markets and it will be necessary to try out a demo account before you actually start trading stocks.

Familiarize yourself with the entire process and ask questions; in this situation, you will never look stupid when you ask questions because you must be up to date with the entire process. Most people are put out by the endless financial jargon associated with stock trading but once you get the gist, you will be able to achieve relative success. The only way to become a successful trader is to keep trading for a lengthy period of time in order for you to collect the information you need to grow and succeed. Take into consideration the different markets that exist as they will be key in your trading success.

A bond may be a regular payment instrument that speaks to a credit created by a money specialist to a receiver (normally a company or legislative). A bond can be speculated of as an I.O.U. amidst the loaner and receiver that comes with the subtleties of the advance and its installments. Bonds are utilized by organizations, districts, states, and autonomous governments to fund ventures and activities. Proprietors of bonds are holders of debt. Bond subtleties incorporate the tip date once the top of the advance is anticipated to be paid to the bondman of affairs and generally incorporates the conditions for variable or mounted intrigue installments created by the receiver.

Bond Issuing

Governments and organizations often utilize bonds to get money. Governments got to finance different development projects within their jurisdictions. The sudden value of war could likewise request the requirement to lift reserves.

So also, organizations can often acquire to develop their business, to get property and devices, to try helpful activities, for innovative work or to enlist representatives. The trouble that big associations keep running into is that they frequently want unquestionably more money than the conventional bank will offer. Bonds offer a fix by enabling varied entity speculators to simply accept the work of the bank. Surely, open obligation markets let an oversized range of monetary specialists every loan a small amount of the capital needed. In addition, markets change loan specialists to supply their bonds to completely different money specialists or to get bonds from different people—long once the primary provision association raised capital.

Bonds are units of company obligation circulated by organizations and designated as tradable resources.

A bond is alluded to as a set regular payment apparatus since bonds usually compensate a set loan fee to debt holders. Variable loan prices are likewise currently terribly traditional.

Bond prices are contrarily related to loan fees: once rates go up, bond prices fall and also the different means around.

Bonds have development dates thus, all things thought-about the chief total should be coated back or hazard default.

How Bonds Work

They are normally alluded to as mounted regular payment securities and are one in all 3 resource categories singular money specialists are usually at home with, aboard stocks (values) and cash reciprocals. Varied company and government bonds are listed on an open market; others are listed clearly over-the-counter (OTC) or on the QT between the receiver and loan specialist.

Whenever organizations or completely different substances got to fund-raise to back new extends, carry on progressing tasks, or renegotiate existing obligations and they will issue bonds licitly to speculators. The receiver (backer) issues a bond that comes with the particulars of the credit, intrigue installments which will be created, and also the time at that the advanced assets (bond head) should be paid back (development date). The premium installment (the coupon) may be a piece of the arrival that bondholders procure for advancing their assets to the surety. The loan value that decides the installment is thought because of the voucher rate.

The underlying value of most bonds is often set at customary, customarily is $100 or $1,000 assumed rate per respective bond. The real market value of a bond banks on upon varied variables: the credit nature of the sponsor, the amount of your time till termination, and also the coupon rate contrasted with the final funding value condition at the time. The assumed rate of the bond is that the factor which will be compensated back to the receiver once the bond develops.

Commonly bonds will be traded off by the underlying investor to completely different money specialists once they need to be been issued. At the tip of the day, a bond speculator does not have to seize a bond utterly through to its development date. It is likewise regular for bonds to be reclaimed by the receiver if funding prices decay, or if the borrower's credit has enhanced, and it will reissue new bonds at a lower value.

Attributes of Bonds

Most bonds share some traditional primary attributes consist of:

Assumed rate is that the money total the bond values at development; it is, in addition, the indicated total the bond surety utilizes once problem-solving premium installments. As an example, say a money specialist buys a bond at a premium $1,090 and another speculator purchases the same bond later once it is mercantilism at a rebate for $980. At the purpose, once the bond develops, the 2 speculators can get the $1,000 presumptive value of the bond.

The coupon rate is that the pace of intrigue the bond sponsor pays on the assumed value of the bond, communicated as a rate. As an example, a five-hitter coupon rate implies that bondholders can get five-hitter x $1000 assumed value = $50 systematically.

Coupon dates are the dates on that the bond sponsor can create intrigue installments. Installments will be created in any interim, but the quality is the period of time installments.

The development date is that the date on that the bond can develop and also the bond sponsor pays the investor the presumptive value of the bond.

The issue value is that the value at that the bond surety at the start sells the bonds.

Two highlights of a bond—credit quality and time to development—are the first determinants of a bond's coupon rate. If the surety encompasses a poor FICO assessment, the danger of default is a lot of distinguished, and these bonds pay a lot of intrigues. Bonds that have an exceptionally long development date likewise ordinarily pay a better loan value.

Bond portfolios can rise or fall in an incentive as funding prices modification. The affectability to changes within the loan fee condition is classed "length". The employment of the term span during this setting is often befuddling to new bond speculators since it does not suggest to the timeframe the bond has before development. Rather, span depicts what proportion a bond's value can rise or fall with associate degree adjustment in funding prices.

The pace of progress of a bond's or bond portfolio's affectability to funding prices (term) is classed "convexity". These variables are troublesome to cipher, and therefore the investigation needed is usually done by specialists.

Bond Classes

There are four essential categories of bonds sold-out within the markets. Be that because it could, you will likewise observe remote bonds issued by organizations and governments on sure stages.

Corporate bonds are issued by organizations. Organizations issue bonds as opposition seek for bank credits for obligation funding by and enormous since bond markets provide increasingly sensible terms and lower loan prices.

City bonds are issued by states and regions. Some civil bonds provide tax-free coupon pay money for money specialists.

Government bonds, for instance, those issued by the U.S. Treasury. Bonds issued by the Treasury with a year or less to development are classified "Bills"; bonds issued with one – ten years to develop are selected "notes"; and bonds issued with over ten years to develop are selected "bonds". The total classification of bonds issued by associate degree administration treasury is frequently all things thought-about alluded to as "treasuries." Government bonds issued by national governments can be alluded to as sovereign obligation.

Office bonds are those issued by government-associated associations, for instance, Fannie Mae or Federal Home Loan Mortgage Corporation.

Bond Assortments

The bonds accessible for money specialists are available in numerous assortments. They will be isolated by the speed or quite intrigue or coupon installment, being reviewed by the patron, or have completely different characteristics.

Zero-coupon bonds do not pay coupon installments to associate degreed rather are issued at a rebate to their customer value that may produce an arrival once the investor is paid the total assumed value once the bond develops. U.S. Treasury bills are a zero-coupon bond. For example, the U.S. Treasury sold-out 26-week bills with $100 presumptive value for $98.78 on Oct eighteenth, 2018. That compares to associate degree absolute yearly yield of 2% once the investor is reimbursed the total $100 at the event date.

Convertible bonds are obligation instruments with associate degree inserted various that allows bondholders to alter over their obligation into stock (value) sooner or later, contingent upon specific conditions just like they provide value. For example, envision a corporation that wants to urge $1 million to finance another enterprise. They may get by supplying bonds with a twelve-tone system coupon that develops in ten years. Be that because it could, if they realized that there have been many money specialists willing to buy bonds with an 8 May 1945 coupon that enabled them to alter over the bond into stock if the stock's price transcended a selected value, they will prefer to issue those.

The bond could the simplest account the organization since they'd have lower intrigue installments whereas the enterprise was in its starting times. If the money specialists modified over their bonds, completely different investors would be weakened, nonetheless the organization wouldn't get to pay, from now on, premium or the pinnacle of the bond.

The speculators UN agency bought a bond might imagine this can be a rare arrangement since they will get pleasure from the face within the stock if the task is effective. They're going out on a limb by tolerating a lower coupon installment, but the potential reward if the bonds are modified over might build that trade-off adequate.

Callable bonds, in addition, have associate degree ingrained alternative but it is completely different than what's found during a bond. A due bond is one that may be "called" back by the organization before it develops. Expect that a corporation has obtained $1 million by supplying bonds with a tenth coupon that develop in 10 years. If loan prices decrease (or the organization's FICO score improves) in year five once the organization might get for 8 May 1945, they're going to revisit to or purchase the bonds from the bondholders for the chief total and reissue new bonds at a lower coupon rate.

A due bond is riskier for the bond buyer because the bond is guaranteed to be known as once it is ascending in value. Remember, once funding prices are falling, bond prices rise. On these lines, due bonds are not as profitable as bonds that are not due with the same development, FICO score, and coupon rate.

A Puttable bond allows the bondholders to place or sell the bond back to the organization before it is developed. This can be profitable for speculators UN agency are stressed that a bond could fall in value, or if they suppose funding prices can rise and that they got to recover their head before the bond falls in value.

The bond patron could incorporate a place various within the bond that blessings the bondholders as a byproduct of a lower coupon rate or simply to incite the bond merchants to create the underlying credit. A placeable bond typically trades at the next incentive than a bond while not a put alternative nonetheless with the same FICO score, development, and coupon rate since it is increasingly profitable to the bondholders.

The potential blends of inserted puts, calls, and interchangeableness rights during a bond are perpetual and everybody is phenomenal. There is positively not associate degree exacting customary for each one in all these rights and many bonds can contain over one form of "choice" which might build correlations troublesome. For the foremost half, singular money specialists rely upon bond specialists to settle on individual bonds or bond supports that meet their contributory objectives.

Evaluating Bonds

The market prices bonds keen about their specific qualities. A bond's price changes systematically, abundant a similar as that of another listed on associate degree open market security, wherever free market activity at no matter minute make sure that watched value. In any case, there is a principle to however bonds are reputable. So far, we've mentioned bonds as if each capitalist holds them to maturity. The facts make sure that if you are doing this you are ensured to recover your head additionally to intrigue; in any case, a bond does not have to be controlled to maturity. Whenever, an investor will sell their bonds within the open market, wherever the value will vacillate, here and there drastically.

The cost of a bond changes as a result of changes in loan fees within the economy. this can be as a result of the approach that for a fixed-rate bond, the patron has vowed to pay a coupon keen about the presumptive value of the bond – thus for a $1,000 customary, 100% yearly bond, the sponsor can pay the investor $100 per annum.

State that common loan fees are likewise 100% at the time that this bond is issued, as controlled by the speed on a fugitive bond. Associate degree capitalist would be indifferent golf stroke resources into the company bond or the administration bond since each would come back $100. In any case, envision once a brief time, that the economy has gotten ugly and loan fees born to five. Presently, the capitalist will simply get $50 from the administration bond, nonetheless would at the present get $100 from the company bond.

This distinction makes the company bond well a lot of seductive. On these lines, investors within the market can offer to the value of the bond till it trades at associate degree exceptional that adjusts the predominant loan fee condition— for this case, the bond can trade at a price of $2,000 in order that the $100 coupon speaks to five. In like manner, if funding prices took off to fifteen, at that time associate degree capitalist might build $150 from the administration bond and wouldn't pay $1,000 to win simply $100. This bond would be sold-out until it found out a price that balanced the yields, for this case to a price of $666.67.

Opposite to Interest Rates

The popular explanation that a bond's value shifts conversely with funding prices works. At the purpose, once loan fees go up, bond prices fall thus on have the impact of evening out the funding value on the bond with winning rates, and therefore the alternative approach around.

Another technique for representing this concept is to have confidence what the yield on our bond would run a price modification, instead of given a loan value modification. For example, if the value were to travel down from a thousand dollars to $800, at that time the yield moves up to 13%. This happens in lightweight of the actual fact that you just are becoming the equivalent ensured $100 on a plus that's value $800 ($100/$800). Then again, if the bond goes up in value to $1,200, the yield to maturity is 9% ($100/$1,200).

Yield-to-Maturity (YTM)

The yield-to-maturity (YTM) of a bond is another technique for pondering a bond's value. Yield to maturity is viewed as a protracted haul bond yield but is communicated as a yearly rate. At the tip of the day, it is the within the pace of comeback of associate degree investment during a bond if the capitalist holds the bond till maturity and if all installments are created as reserved. YTM may be a remarkable computation nonetheless is incredibly valuable as a plan assessing the participating quality of 1 bond in regard to completely different bonds of various coupon and maturity within the market. The instruction for YTM includes unraveling for the funding value within the concomitant condition, that isn't an easy assignment, and during this approach, most bond investors impressed by YTM can utilize a PC:

Yield to Maturity Formula

We can likewise quantify the foretold changes in bond prices given associate degree adjustment in loan prices with a life referred to as the length of a bond. The term is communicated in units of the number of years since it at the start alluded to zero-coupon bonds, whose span is its maturity.

For helpful functions, in any case, length speaks to the worth modification during a bond given the tenth modification in funding prices. We have a tendency to name this second, an increasingly viable definition of the changed length of a bond.

The length is often determined to choose the worth affectability to loan fee adjustments of a solitary bond, or for a meeting of diverse bonds. Once all is claimed in done, bonds with long developments, and what is more bonds with low vouchers have the simplest affectability to funding value changes. The risks associated with bonds are complex and this means that the length changes when rates and costs change, as well.

Chapter 7: Strategies and Tactics

Day trading frameworks are essential when you want to benefit by unending, little esteem advancements. The solid, feasible methodology relies upon start to finish a particular examination, utilizing charts, pointers and guides to predict potential worth improvements. This page will offer you a concentrated relief down of beginners trading strategies, functioning beyond what many would consider possible up to the front line, mechanized and even asset-specific frameworks.

It will similarly plot some regional differences to think about, similarly as directing you to some important resources. Finally, be that as it may, you will need to find a multi-day trading philosophy that suits you.

How Beginners can Start Trading

Before you get slowed down in a staggering universe of incredibly particular markers, revolve around the stray pieces of a direct day trading framework. Numerous people wrongly think they need an extraordinarily tangled framework to succeed intraday, yet as often as possible the more straightforward, the more fruitful.

The Basics

Consolidate the significant parts underneath into your system.

The money the administrators – Before you start, plunk down and pick the sum you are willing to risk. Bear at the highest point of the need rundown best traders will not place capital of more than two percent remaining in a precarious situation for each trade. You have to set yourself up for specific setbacks if you have to connect with when the triumphs start coming in.

Time the load up – Profit cannot come if you simply allow some time consistently to trading. You need to consistently screen the markets and be vigilant for trade openings.

Start nearly nothing – As you find your feet, stick to the furthest reaches of three stocks in an alone day. It is more intelligent to get extraordinary at a couple than to be ordinary and making no money on weights.

Preparing – Comprehending market complexities isn't adequate, you furthermore need to stay instructed? Guarantee you keep conscious to date with market news and any events that will influence your advantage, for instance, a shift in financial methodology. You can find a bounty of online financial and business resources that will keep you mindful of everything.

Consistency – It is more difficult than it plans to monitor sentiments when you are five coffees and you have been looking at the screen for a significant long time. You need to let figures, reason and your approach control you, not fear.

Timing – The market can get flimsy when it opens each day and remembering that cultivated casual speculators may most likely scrutinize the models and advantage, you should stick around for your opportunity. So hold down for the underlying 15 minutes, notwithstanding all that you have hours ahead.

Notwithstanding whether you are after mechanized day trading methods, or juvenile and moved techniques, you will need to think about three central fragments; unsteadiness, liquidity, and volume. If you are to benefit on little esteem improvements, picking the right stock is basic. These three segments will empower you to choose that decision.

Liquidity – It engages you to swiftly enter and leave trades at a charming and steady expense. Liquid product techniques, for example, will focus on gold, grungy oil and vaporous oil.

Shakiness – This uncovers to you your potential advantage expand. The more critical the insecurity, the more noticeable advantage or setback you may make. The cryptographic money market is an example of a model comprehended for high eccentrics.

Volume – This estimation will uncover how frequently the asset is trading within a specific time period. For casual speculators, it is generally called 'ordinary consistently trading volume.' High volume tells you there is considerable energy for the favorable position. A development in volume is normally a marker worth increases or decreases.

Day trading philosophy

1. Breakout

These philosophies rotate round when the price moves from a definite point on the chart. The breakout dealer goes into a lengthy function after the gain or security breaks above resistance. Then again, you enter a short position as soon as the inventory breaks.

After a favorable role or security trades previous the unique price limit, insecurity basically additions and fees will typically incline toward the breakout.

It is necessary to discover the right trading instruments. Keep in mind the top of the priority list the advantage's help and opposition levels. Much of the time, the fee has hit these centers and they become greater.

Section Points

This phase is now not too horrific and clear. Costs set to shut or more impediments need a bearish position. Costs set to shut and need a bullish position.

Plan your routes out

Use the advantage's progressing introduction to increase a sensible objective. Using chart fashions will make this approach a good deal progressively accurate. You can figure the common continuous really worth swings to make a target. If the typical really worth swing has been 3 over the span of the remaining a couple of considerable worth swings, this would be a sensible target. When you have touched base at that target you can leave the alternate and value the advantage.

2. Scalping

One of the most incredible frameworks is scalping. It is in particular properly recognized in the forex market, and it would like to pick up by minute really worth changes. The central motive is the sum. You will prefer to sell when the exchange winds up advantageous. This is a rapid paced and invigorating way to deal with trade, yet it will in customary be risky. You need a high buying and selling chance to strive to out the for the most section secure versus repay extent.

Be attentive for flimsy instruments, attractive liquidity and be warm on timing. You can barely wait for the market, you need to shut dropping trades as speedy as time grants.

Pervasive scalping trading device

3. Energy

Energy is an important element for understanding success in stock trading. On the other hand, you can blur the value drop. Along these lines round your value target is when volume begins to decrease. This methodology is straightforward and viable if utilized accurately. Be that as it may, you should guarantee you're mindful of up and coming news and profit declarations. Only a couple of moments on each trade will have a significant effect on your part of the arrangement.

4. Reversal

But intensely examined and possibly unsafe when used through fledglings, rearrange buying and selling is used anyplace all through the world. It is commonly called example trading, pull back drifting and a imply reversal methodology.

This machine contradicts critical basis as you intend to change against the example. You ought to most probable precisely perceive manageable pullbacks, however, predict their quality. To do this correctly you want all-round market data and experience.

The 'step via step pivot' method is seen as a captivating incidence of pivot trading because it centers around obtaining as well as selling the step by means of step low and high switches.

5. Using Pivot Points

Understanding the most efficient way of using your pivot points will make all the difference in your trade. The pivot point will identify different fundamental aspects of your trade, and this information is invaluable if you want to make profits. The pivot point will enable you to calculate appropriate stop-loss measures, the entry points of trade as well as their exit. Without a pivot point, you might fall in the common trap of allowing a successful trade to continue even as the trend is changing.

For instance, if you have maximized on a bearish trade but there is evidence that the trade will soon turn, it is useful to have a pivot point. It will help you curtail your 'greed' so that you can come out of the trade while you are still on top. This is important because you will have to understand the important parts of the trade that you must pay attention to and prevent a successful trade from suddenly turning sour.

Minimizing Losses

A stop-loss is a limit you set in order to prevent a trade that is going bad from making any more losses. A stop-loss is like an acknowledgment that the trade is likely to go bad, and so you set a point in which you can stomach the loss. For instance, if you want to invest in a bearish market with the product at a price of $88, you can set the stop-loss at $87 just in case things go bad. This means you will lose a dollar per unit of your investment on the trade if things go south because the price can even drop to zero within a short amount of time.

Stop-losses are a reprieve for beginners because they prevent all their money from being wiped out the first time. Chances are that you will latch on your first few trades and one of them will go against your anticipation. At this point, it is appropriate to set the stop-loss so as to set the maximum loss point for the trade. This ensures that you do not lose the entirety of your investment but instead have a chance to trade on in the future.

Forex Trading Strategies

Digital currency Trading Strategies

The empowering and eccentric cryptographic cash market presents a ton of possibilities to make money. It might seem complicated at first, but if you do your research well, you will be surprised that it can be a viable source of money for the long term.

Strategies for Stock Trading

Day trading procedures for shares depend upon endless comparative fashions plot all via this page, and you can use and vast parcel of the philosophies unfold out above. Underneath anyway is a precise framework you can follow to the stock market.

Spread Betting Strategies

Spread making a bet empowers you to conjecture on infinite average markets except ever absolutely owning the advantage. Also, strategies are typically immediate.

Moving Average Crossover

There are three moving normal lines:

Position: 20 durations – the brisk moving normal

Position: 60 intervals – the moderate moving regular

Position: 100 intervals – the instance pointer

This is one of the moving midpoints strategies that make a buy sign when the rapid-moving everyday indicator crosses the average transferring typical. A sell signal is delivered in fact when the quick transferring standard crosses below the moderate transferring ordinary.

Along these lines, you will open enable a position as the moving normal line crosses a solitary way and you will close the position when it crosses again the contrary way.

In what manner may you develop there may be an example? You recognize the instance is on if the worth bar stays above or below the hundred-time allotment line.

CFD Strategies

Working up a sensible day trading framework can be tangled. Regardless, settle on an instrument, for instance, a CFD and your movement can also be somewhat extra straightforward.

CFDs are harassed over the difference between the entry points of a trade. Their dominance has only been increasing with time. This is on the grounds that you can benefit when the trade is beneficial, moving in the anticipated direction while never owning the fundamental resource.

Regional Differences

Various markets go with exceptional shots and deterrents to endure. Day trading methodology for the Japanese market can also no longer be as effective when you try in a different place. For example, a couple of international locations can also the uncertainty of the news, so the market might also not react also as you would foresee that they ought to be returned home.

Rules have to be considered carefully because frameworks may be redone to suit inner, unique guidelines, for instance, the highest least value changes in edge accounts. Along these lines, leap on the web and take a look at cloud rules may not affect your framework before you stash away your merited cash.

You may additionally discover one of a kind countries have exceptional price escape conditions to soar through. If you are organized in the West anyway need to apply your average day buying and selling frameworks in another area of the world, you need to whole your work first.

What assessment do you have to pay for? Is it a must to pay it overseas or maybe locally? Fringe value dissimilarities should have a sizeable impact on your piece of the deal.

Risk Management

Stop-loss

A stop-loss prevents you from losing money if your trade has gone in the opposite direction to what you were expecting. For instance, if you were trading in anticipation of it being a bullish market but it is actually bearish, a stop-loss will prevent your trade from being active from a specific point that you specify.

For instance, if it was your intention to go upwards on a currency with a value of $76 but it actually goes down to $73, you can set up your stop-loss at$75 to minimize any losses on such a trade.

Position size

This describes the number of offers you can make on a single trade. It is necessary o first consult with the forex trading platform on the actual size you can take, but it is possible to put thousands of offers. For instance, if you are trading a certain currency whose entrance point value is $102 with a stop loss set at $100, then the risk at this point is $2.

Learning Methods

There is no single way of learning because everybody has their own way of processing information. Therefore, as much as you get lots of advice online on how to trade in the most efficient way, the best thing to actually do is develop your own trading routine based on your strengths. If you can achieve this, you will always be able to process advice in a feasible manner in order to guide your trades to be successful ones.

Online diaries

If you are scanning for the high-quality buying and selling methodology that works, online locales are the spot to go. Much of the time, you can learn interior day systems and extra knowledge from skilled traders. What's more, online diaries are an extra special wellspring of inspiration.

Social occasions

A few people will gain the best from gatherings. This is on the grounds that you can remark and pose inquiries. In addition, you regularly discover day trading strategies so natural anybody can utilize. In any case, because of the restricted space, you typically just get the rudiments of day trading systems. In this way, if you are searching for additional inside and out systems, you might need to consider other sources of information.

PDFs

These have become extremely important sources of information for anybody seeking precise information. It is possible for an individual to include lots of information in a PDF file that will incorporate diagrams and other visual aids to bring the information to life.

Another favorable reason is that they are so easy to find. For example, you can discover helpful PDFs with a simple Google search that helps you identify the topic and any other important keyword.

Besides, you will discover they are furnished in the direction of merchants of all experience levels. Therefore, it is possible to find the right kind of PDF for your forex trading needs regardless of your trading experience.

Online Courses

Different human beings will discover instinctive and sorted information sources that will enable them to learn. Fortunately, there are spots online that provide such benefits. You can locate training material on day trading websites that will be extremely useful.

Trading as the Main Source of Income

Should you consider quitting your job and begin day trading for profit, then you have a hard, stimulating ride before you. You will have to work just as hard as you are at your current job, making it difficult for you to do other things. It becomes your full-time job and it is one you should fully remain focused on.

Your piece of the deal will depend vastly on the structures your use. Along these lines, it justifies recollecting that it is as often as possible the instantaneous methodology that suggests productive, paying little note to whether you are enthusiastic about any type of investment.

Also, recall that specialized examination ought to be an extensive exercise in aiding your philosophy. Likewise, paying attention to whether you pick out the early phase or a different trade, controlling your threat is crucial if you have to make money in a successful way. Eventually, growing a philosophy that is favorable will always take time; Remember, patience is a virtue.

Chapter 8: Investing for Long term Growth

While the stock market is filled with vulnerability, certain time tested standards can enable investors to support their odds for long haul achievement.

The graph below shows the best approaches towards investing for long term growth;

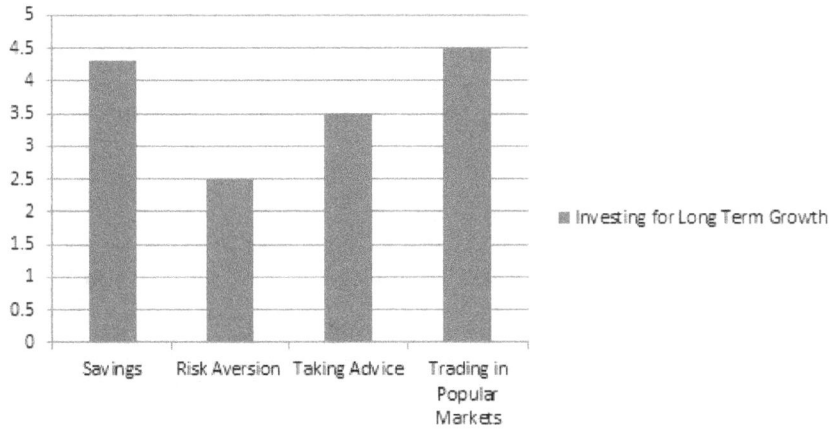

There are various approaches to investing in the long term. One of them is through savings; this approach focuses on putting aside lots of money whether through joint contributions or locking away the profits from an investment. This is an excellent approach to planning for the long term because it allows the investor to have a large pool of funds to live their lives freely. Savings has always been the first and most straightforward approach to living in a debt-free manner and should be considered as a way of planning from the long term.

The best savings accounts to use are fixed deposit accounts that do not allow you to withdraw your money for a specific duration of time. As long as you keep the account active and make constant deposits, your savings grow and can be unlocked at a pre-determined point in the future. This is a collected method of ensuring that you have a large amount of money to handle your needs in the future and also to handle the soaring rates of inflation. If you want to think long term, then always save money in order for it to be available as a source of capital in the future.

Another suitable long-term investment strategy is having a large risk aversion. This is for the person who does not have a progressive portfolio and wants to maintain a certain level of capital. The action to take in this case is to ensure that the capital remains relatively similar to reflect current inflation rates. This type of portfolio will attract very little expenses while attracting a large amount of income and retaining of the initial investment. Risk aversion prevents large capital outlays and ensures that there is always a source of capital available in preceding ideas for whatever projects you might have in mind.

A high-risk aversion is a typical quality of several investors who are looking to significantly cut their losses and guarantee constant cash flow. It is an important objective to have because it empowers the investor to maintain lucrative investments that are always profitable when the maturity date arrives. Long term investments usually have very large pay-offs when they mature to success and it justifies the amount of time it takes for an investment to truly grow. Observing these simple strategies for ensuring growth guarantees that there is always capital; this is because it is exposed to very little risk.

The strategy of taking advice might seem negligible but it is extremely important when looking for long term investments. Taking advice empowers you to follow important trends that are currently profitable and enables you to join in the act. This is an excellent learning point for any novice because they can witness first-hand from seasoned professionals the strategies to use and the markets to exploit. Taking advice might at first seem cumbersome when you begin investing, but if you have long term goals, listen to those who are already doing it.

The advice of people gives you the advantage of sharing their experiences. Thus, they will guide you to appropriate investment opportunities where you can take a lesson or two about investing your own money. You will learn fundamental aspects of long term investing, some that are just usually mired in financial jargon. Before long, you will have a comprehensive understanding of the different trading approaches and you will be in a position to make decisions based on the knowledge you have actually acquired. Listen to what the experts have to say and follow different information sources on the internet as it will give you good guidance in the direction to follow to invest in the long term.

One more strategy that is important to remember is that trading in the right markets makes all the difference. Investing, too in the right markets allows you to focus on what you really are good at and creates a constant income stream. When you are in the right markets, it is possible to truly understand what is going on and place yourself in a position to profit. Remember that you have the advantage of knowledge over some other investors and this should give you the upper hand when it comes to exploiting opportunities.

While you should limit charge obligation, accomplishing significant yields is the essential objective.

At the point when most starting investors think about the stock market, they think about the quick-paced purchasing and selling of stocks to make speedy benefits. While trading (moving resources, for example, stocks, to make a benefit on the deal) is one approach to approach contributing, it isn't the main way.

Traders for the most part attempt to profit by momentary changes in the market by as often as possible purchasing and selling offer dependent on patterns.

Trading can be viewed as involving the furthest edge of the range from long haul contributing. The objectives of most investors will be best met by an increasing preservationist (and less dynamic) approach. In any case, once more, everything comes down to what your objectives are.

Before You Pick Stocks

You need cash to contribute that does not restrain your capacity to meet other financial needs.

You should be eager to lose a few (and in all respects inconsistently, all) of that cash.

The riskier the investment, the higher the potential misfortunes and prizes.

Trading (market timing) is extremely difficult to do. You must be correct twice — when you purchase the stock and again when you sell it. Indeed, even experts with long periods of experience considerable difficulties profiting along these lines.

Picking Stocks — an Art, Not a Science

You can encounter the energy of picking stocks and following their advancement without the emotional good and bad times of consistent dynamic trading. The most significant thing to recollect is that there is no enchantment recipe to profiting in the stock market. Indeed, even the most prepared investors pick their stock investments utilizing hypotheses or procedures, with shifting degrees of achievement, contingent upon a wide scope of factors.

Bear and bull

Bulls and Bears

You may have heard the terms bull and bear markets. In the least difficult terms, bull means rising and bear means declining.

Along these lines, if you are bullish on a specific stock, it implies that you accept its worth is expanding. If somebody says it is a bear market they imply that the markets are going descending.

Stock Analysis Methods

Investors depend on different strategies for assessing the future estimation of stock. A few models include:

Key Analysis Qualitative Analysis Technical Analysis
Two Common Stock-Picking Strategies
Stock ticker rising

The factors that decide if the stock market or individual stocks go up or down, for the most part, can't be anticipated, so investors have built up a few techniques for figuring out what to put resources into. Here are only two models:

Worth Investing includes discovering organizations that are trading for short of what they as of now value.
Development Investing means discovering organizations that you accept will develop sooner rather than later.
Worth Investing

With worth contributing, you need to observe organizations that hope to be underestimated in the present market. Utilizing your picked technique or blend of strategies, (for example, breaking down basics or subjective factors) to decide an organization's worth, you would pick stocks that appear to be a decent deal at their present cost.

Development Investing

Instead of searching for stocks that presently are underestimated, development investors search for indicators, (for example, income per share and the value profit proportion) that a stock will develop later on. This technique can support new items or development ventures −, for example, new advances − that the investor accepts will develop.

Before you surge out to purchase your first stocks, you will need to do further investigation into these and different strategies all alone or with a financial organizer to decide the best approach depends on your risk tolerance, courses of events and extraordinary contributing objectives.

A Note on Loss

When you are simply beginning contributing, recollect that misfortune on paper is different from a real misfortune. During the financial emergency of 2008, numerous investors hauled cash out of their investments; be that as it may, numerous different investors trusted that the markets will recoup and made up a few or the majority of their misfortunes. "Enduring it" for a misfortune to recoup here and there is − and in some cases isn't — the best methodology, in light of the basics of the investment. Work with a confided in financial counsel to assess your best procedure.

Chapter 9: Risk, Money management & Volatility

Cash the executives is the represent the deciding moment range of abilities that will affect a trader's life span the most. Regardless of how in fact talented a trader might be, poor cash the board can cause a wide range of unforced blunders bringing about record blow-ups. Cash the board involves overseeing risk and influence. The influence part is the place the threat is the best. Regardless of whether a trader has an 80% success rate, poor cash the executives on the 20% can crash the record. Though a trader with a 60% success rate can even now stay entirely productive with solid cash the executives' aptitudes. Legitimate cash the executives is constantly a work in advancement that is controlled by understanding, discipline, reasonability, readiness and passionate control. Here are 7 cash the board tips for day trading.

Cut Your Risks

It tends to entice to press higher risk trades by taking a lot bigger offer positions or tossing a "Hail Mary" type grand slam swing. Typically these sorts of trades are removed from edginess to make back huge misfortunes and these end up gravely for the trader. The market has the uncanny capacity to win during high-risk trades. This is on the grounds that the market comprehends that these trades depend on feelings and edginess. It is human instinct to battle back and goes heavier when taking misfortunes, not a different way.

Understanding this idea will assist you in identifying high-risk trade circumstances and maintain a strategic distance from them. At the point when a trader has a progression of losing trades, the proper activity is to trim down offers or potentially quit if max everyday dollar misfortune levels are hit. Keep in mind, it just takes one terrible over-utilized trade to prompt a record victory.

If you are new to a specific trading arrangement or thinking about trading a profoundly unpredictable stock, ensure you are sure and have an idiot-proof trading plan set up.

Focus on Risk-Reward Ratio

Preceding pulling the trigger on a trade set-up, measure the potential benefit versus the stop-misfortune on the trade. Normally, this is the risk/remunerate proportion where the potential misfortune is contrasted with the potential benefit. The customary believing is to consistently have at any rate a 2 to 1 proportion of remuneration to risk (in a perfect world, closer to 3:1 or higher). Be that as it may, there is another factor that makes maybe the most material effect on the proportion. That is a likelihood.

What is the likelihood that the reward will hit before the stop-misfortune is hit? If the upside is equivalent to the stop-misfortune, yet the likelihood for hitting the upside initially is above 80%, at that point the trade might be legitimate for an accuracy hawker with control. In any case, if the order to take the littler benefit isn't directed, would you be able to assume a stop-misfortune? This is the place a trader can get injured. The most ideal approach to raise likelihood is by diminishing the benefit target while sifting more grounded example set-ups. If the chances at a + 0.20 cost move are above 80%, at that point an equivalent − 0.20 stop-misfortune bodes well on this 1 for 1 risk/remunerate trade. Estimating the likelihood of an objective being hit depends on the quality of the basic example and timing the passage and exits appropriately.

Avoid Averaging Down

There is a difference between scaling into a place that was pre-reflected and averaging down on a misfortune that wasn't anticipated. This tip applies to the last mentioned. Each trader should know the qualification between the two. Averaging down from a place of shortcoming without an arrangement is a surefire approach to victory a record. In these circumstances, a trader midpoints down out of urgency and expectation. The issue is two-overlap.

To start with, if by a supernatural occurrence, the trade works out and the trader leaves with a benefit, it sets a risky point of reference that when in peril, he should simply twofold down. This is a street to destroy in the long run. Besides, if the trade does not return, at that point the outcome can be enormous misfortunes and potentially constrained liquidation edge calls. Traders should initially consider assuming the stop-misfortune as opposed to averaging down as a rule. Use stop misfortunes to purchase time and take the strain burden off your shoulders. At exactly that point would you be able to consider an increasingly exact reemergence or inversion trade or simply move onto another stock.

Do Not Trade with Retaliation in Mind

A great many people will concur that having a benefit and afterward losing it is more regrettable than failing to have made the benefit in any case. For what reason is that? The inner self. They should be correct is imbued in our mind. It is anything but a matter of being a showoff or shallow. The mind consistently looks for straightforwardness and the decrease of pressure and strain as in the Cognitive Dissonance hypothesis by Festinger. The need to 'make things right' is the thing that can intuitively compel a trigger to attempt to make back the misfortunes and lose the feeling of rationale and objectivity all the while. The term retribution intends to establish vengeance to 'even' or balance things back to ordinary. It is an inborn blemish that the market would like to abuse. In this manner, it is significant that traders perceive when the retribution trading kicks in and promptly pull the off button. Retaliation trading sets a terrible point of reference and at last, can be deadly to your record.

Rest

A trader's brain research stamina is significant in staying adaptable and the capacity to make great convenient decisions and responses. To remain new, it is a smart thought to portion the trading inside the day and remove ordinary breaks from the screen. When you gaze at a screen throughout the day consistently, the psyche does not stop working or being affected. The mental way to deal with trading can depend on the physical. This way to physically break the association, get up from your seat and leave for a strong break somewhere in the range of 10 moments to a few hours. This is the best way to renew the psychological fuel measure.

You may likewise locate that taking breaks from trading for longer timeframes can help give you the "invigorate" you need. Taking breaks, particularly after a major misfortune or win, can enable you to clear your brain and return to trading taking care of business.

Stop-Losses are Important

This takes order to manage. If conceivable, having the trading stage trigger the maximum day by day stop is regularly the most ideal approach to regulate. Consistently trader ought to be jumpy and realize that it is consistent that one hiding trade that is fit for setting off a progression of occasions to push him into smothering his record. More often than not, it is a peculiarity or remarkable stock move that structures, which sucks the trader in on an inappropriate side. If the trader does not acknowledge the irregularity, it can and will frequently swallow him step by step from the outset and after that trap him.

The maximum dollar sum should extend between a few times the normal everyday benefits if the trader keeps up an 80%

success/misfortune proportion. If the exactness rate drops, at that point, the maximum misfortune should drop too. This sort of proportion puts exceptional consideration on the precision rate. This functions admirably for accuracy hawkers.

Focus on Your Niche Area

Each trader has a trading style (technique, kinds of stocks and plays) which they are most alright with. The stunt is finding what they are without becoming penniless. The mix of the previously mentioned aspects is the thing that creates your specialty. When you discover your specialty, stick with it and be mindful so as not to stray. When you can identify your specialty, it is reasonable to stay with that specialty until it is never again a specialty. Inevitably, the straightforwardness gets uncovered in this way successfully closing the lucky opening to benefit. Thusly, when a specialty is discovered, it is ideal to profit by that specialty until it winds up immersed or too straightforward, typically both.

Never place a trade exclusively to compensate for another trade. Nobody preferences managing misfortunes, yet it is significant that traders stay reasonable.

Chapter 10: The Importance of Diversifying

Diversification is a strategy that diminishes risk by apportioning investments among different financial instruments, businesses, and different classes. It expects to expand returns by putting resources into different zones that would each respond differently to a similar occasion.

Most investment experts concur that, in spite of the fact that it does not ensure against misfortune, diversification is the most significant segment of arriving at long-extend financial objectives while limiting risk. Here, we take a gander at why this is valid and how to achieve diversification in your portfolio.

- Diversification diminishes risk by putting resources into investments that length different financial instruments, enterprises, and different classifications.
- Risk can be both undiversifiable or foundational, and diversifiable or unsystemic.
- Investors may discover adjusting a diversified portfolio confused and costly, and it might accompany lower rewards in light of the fact that the risk is alleviated.
- Different Types of Risk

- Investors defy two fundamental kinds of risk when contributing. The first is undiversifiable, which is otherwise called efficient or market risk. This kind of risk is related to each organization. Normal causes incorporate expansion rates, exchange rates, political flimsiness, war, and financing costs. This kind of risk isn't specific to a specific organization or industry, and it can't be disposed of or diminished through diversification—it is only a risk investor must acknowledge.

Methodical risk influences the market completely, not only one specific investment vehicle or industry.

The second sort of risk is diversifiable. This risk is otherwise called unsystematic risk and is specific to an organization, industry, market, economy, or nation. It very well may be decreased through diversification. The most widely recognized wellsprings of unsystematic risk are business risk and financial risk. Hence, the point is to put resources into different resources so they won't all be influenced a similar route by market occasions.

Why You Should Diversify

Suppose you have an arrangement of just carrier stocks. If it is declared that aircraft pilots are going on an inconclusive strike and that all flights are dropped, share costs of carrier stocks will drop. That implies your portfolio will encounter a perceptible drop in worth.

If, be that as it may, you counteracted aircraft industry stocks with two or three railroad stocks, just piece of your portfolio would be influenced. Truth be told, there is a decent shot the railroad stock costs would move, as travelers go to trains as an elective type of transportation.

In any case, you could diversify significantly further in light of the fact that there are numerous risks that influence both rail and air in light of the fact that each is engaged with transportation. An occasion that decreases any type of movement harms the two sorts of organizations. Analysts, for instance, would state that rail and air stocks have a solid relationship.

By diversifying, you are ensuring you do not place all your investments tied up in one place.

Hence, you would need to diversify in all cases, different kinds of organizations as well as different sorts of businesses. The more uncorrelated your stocks are, the better.

It is additionally essential to diversify among different resource classes. Different resources, for example, bonds and stocks won't respond similarly to unfriendly occasions. A blend of benefit classes will diminish your portfolio's affectability to market swings. By and large, bond and value markets move in inverse ways, so if your portfolio is diversified crosswise over the two zones, upsetting developments in a single will be balanced by positive outcomes in another.

Lastly, remember the area, area, area. Diversification likewise implies you should search for investment openings past your own land outskirts. All things considered, unpredictability in the United States may not influence stocks and bonds in Europe, so putting resources into that piece of the world may limit and balance the risks of contributing at home.

Issues with Diversification

While there are numerous advantages to diversification, there might be a few drawbacks also. It might be to some degree unwieldy to deal with a diverse portfolio, particularly if you have numerous possessions and investments. Besides, it can place a mark in your bottom line. Not all investment vehicles cost the equivalent, so purchasing and selling might be costly— from exchange expenses to financier charges. What's more, since higher risk accompanies higher prizes, you may wind up restricting what you turn out with.

There are likewise extra sorts of diversification, and numerous engineered investment items have been made to oblige investors' risk tolerance levels. Notwithstanding, these components can be exceptionally confounded and are not designed to be formed by novice or little investors. For the individuals who have less investment experience, and do not have the financial sponsorship to go into supporting exercises, bonds are the most well-known approach to diversify against the stock market.

Shockingly, even the best investigation of an organization and its financial articulations can't promise it won't be a losing investment. Diversification won't counteract a disadvantage, yet it can diminish the result of misrepresentation and terrible data on your portfolio.

What number of Stocks You Should Have?

Clearly, belonging five stocks is exceptional to owning one, yet there comes a moment that adding more stocks to your portfolio stops to have any types of effect. There is a discussion over what number of stocks are expected to diminish risk while keeping up an exceptional yield.

The most traditional view contends that an investor can accomplish ideal diversification with just 15 to 20 stocks spread crosswise over different businesses.

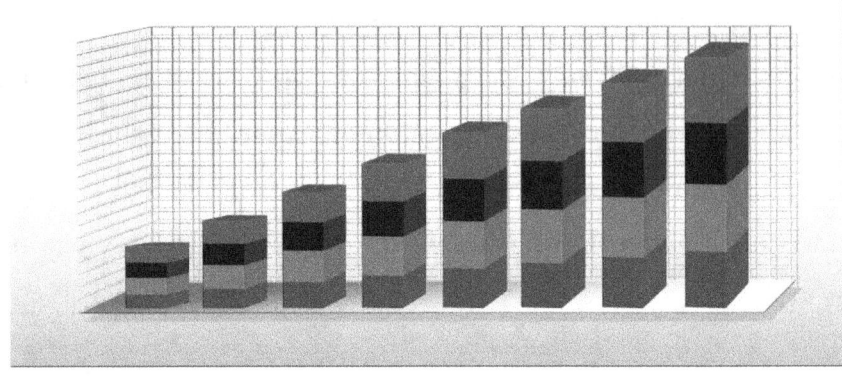

Diversification can enable an investor to oversee risk and diminish the unpredictability of an advantage's value developments. Keep in mind, in any case, that regardless of how diversified your portfolio is, risk can never be dispensed with totally.

You can diminish the risk related with individual stocks, however, broad market risks influence almost every stock thus it is additionally essential to diversify among different resource classes. The key is to locate an upbeat medium among risk and return. This guarantees you can accomplish your financial objectives while as yet getting a decent night's rest.

Chapter 11: Portfolio Ideas

Just as it is important for collecting information and specializing in specific trades, it is also important to have a well-kept portfolio that can guarantee you success in your trades. A properly assessed portfolio takes into consideration numerous factors that guarantee the success of any endeavor. When finances are properly organized, it becomes possible for the investor to understand what needs to be done in order to achieve success in the investment opportunity. A good portfolio guarantees minimal risks are incurred by the investor while maximizing on available opportunities to ensure success.

There are many sources of information one can exploit for portfolio ideas; to begin with, taking advice from expert traders is extremely important if you want to succeed. This is because the experiences of others can significantly help you minimize specific losses that will otherwise take you down. It is important to always factor in the experiences of others who have traded in markets that you aspire to trade in for crucial advice. What they tell you can easily help you make crucial decisions on the type of portfolio you want and how you will maintain it. Take advice from anybody who has already engaged in the stock market as they will have useful information on the different types of portfolios.

Another source of information on portfolio ideas is the internet. It is possible for you to collect a host of information that will specify different aspects of trading and enable you to develop an appropriate portfolio. If you are patient, you should go through several different websites because there is a host of information on different ideas you can exploit in order to build up your portfolio. You will also find the experiences of others on the internet and this is an important source of information for you.

You can also get portfolio ideas from professionals, but the one drawback is that you are likely to spend a lot of money. Asset and finance managers in major institutions are in a position to offer you a wealth of information as well as the support of their institutions. Their aim is to ensure that they can make you a customer while helping you build your portfolio at a cost. However, their levels of investment are tremendous as compared to the novice trader and they are likely to offer you appropriate guidelines that will be instrumental in helping you trade successfully.

You can also rely on your own experience to get portfolio ideas, but the only way to truly exploit your experience is by trading on demo accounts. Instead of making losses and mistakes as you seek portfolio ideas, do it virtually with virtual money so that you can understand the advantages as well as pitfalls of trading. When you use a demo account, you safeguard yourself from losses and give yourself an opportunity to learn as much as possible. The advantage of demo accounts is that you can transfer some of the knowledge acquired into your trading strategies to ensure they align with your objectives.

Once you have gathered portfolio ideas, your next challenge is to implement them appropriately so that you can start profiting from your trades appropriately. One of the most important things you must have in mind is that a well-diversified portfolio is your avenue to success. A portfolio that specifically focuses on single categories of assets will not yield much particularly if a trade collapses. A single trade gone badly can affect an entire portfolio that does not have appropriate diversification and this can be very dangerous when looking to maintain a source of income.

One of the most important things to start off with is the asset allocation for your portfolio. The importance of understanding this is because it clarifies your objectives for your assets and also determines the amount of risk you are willing to take when trading. The objectives of your trade play an important part in determining your investment approach and your overall projected profitability. When you first start with asset allocation, you are in a position to set your portfolio in preparation for the implementation of a plan that will benefit you.

There are a number of critical ways that you can modify your portfolio to ensure that it is appropriate for achieving your objectives;

You can decide on a Preservationist portfolio that emphasizes maintaining the current state of the capital. Profits are incurred from salary payments, interest payments and profits on matured bonds. It is a portfolio for the investor who is thinking more in the long term than in the short and it offers excellent rewards, for example, after ten years. This type of portfolio insists on always maintaining the current state of the capital until the maturity period when the owner can decide what to do with it.

The other type of portfolio that you can consider is the Progressive portfolio. This emphasizes on taking high risks and investing a large part of the capital on value. This type of investor also likes to pool their resources in other common financial agreements to increase the capital outlay and also spread the risk of the business. This type of portfolio is aggressive and a large part of the capital is used for funding the entire investment. The advantage of this approach is that as high risks are concerned, rewards are usually high and the owner can start reaping benefits within a year of the business.

The next step is to organize the portfolio so that you can allocate your resources appropriately. There are many methods in which you can achieve a portfolio; one such method is through common funds and they entail the owner having bonds and stocks picked for them by reserve directors. Another method of achieving a portfolio is through stock picking where an appropriate way of getting the right stocks to be selected is done. Other methods include bond picking and Exchange-Traded Funds. This way, you set up your portfolio appropriately in order for it to reflect your stated goals.

There are numerous risks associated with portfolio ideas, and so you must state your goals early enough and clearly. For instance, you need to decide whether your goals are short term or long term because there are appropriate strategies for each one of them. If you are able to determine your needs and you set up an appropriate plan, you can have a portfolio reflecting one of the two as stated above. The right portfolio idea for you will ultimately depend on your risk aversion and the time period you intend to have to make an investment.

You also need to have an adequate capital reserve in order to make your portfolio functional. For the investments you intend to make, it is necessary to maintain a standard capital threshold, even in value on the investment in order to avoid the risks associated with making losses. A good capital reserve ensures that you always have a stop-gap in case the initial investment fails; you can learn from your mistakes and still remain on course to achieving your objectives by understanding the pitfalls. Thereafter, you will be able to understand your own portfolio without your financial manager's help as it expands and aligns with your intentions.

Choose the right markets as this is very important when looking to make a profit. Some people choose a market simply because they have heard of it and it can be catastrophic when looking to make large-scale changes. Trading in the right market is instrumental in ensuring that you can maintain an optimum level of risk aversion and you can continue gaining knowledge in that specific niche. When you start understanding different options, it becomes possible to maintain your portfolio as you envision and it will be a key source of finance for other projects that you might intend to start.

The right portfolio idea must reflect the values of your investment strategy by timing and market penetration. As your stock grows, your own knowledge and understanding of the system must, as well. This will possibly mean interacting with the financial giants of your niche and they will introduce you to their methods of trading that will bring you closer to them. Do not remain very far from the words of advice of professionals who have been doing it for a long time because it will enable them to put you in a position of power.

The right portfolio ideas always incorporate different strategies as a form of security. It is important to come up with multiple plans because they will act as a stop-gap to a failed plan. What should be clear through all the plans is your objectives, but always have a plan B if necessary. Sometimes after a proper assessment of a stock market, you might spot two different trends and capitalize on both of them will always be a good idea. Come up with different plans as they will give you an entirely different perspective on the approaches you should have when trading. Always be prepared and it should be an important motto when looking through portfolio ideas to determine the best options to utilize.

Chapter 12: The Most Important Mistakes That Beginners Make

Numerous beginners start trading with high benefit desires, yet discover decently fast that creation cash reliably isn't as simple as they anticipated. For a few, this acknowledgment can be very disheartening, especially in light of the fact that there are not many interests that encourage deep feelings as considerably as trading.

In truth, errors are not just reserved to novices, but experts, too, have made such grave errors that some of them have stopped trading. The way to their inevitable achievement, in any case, is that the experts study their missteps and figure out how to limit them going ahead. It is good to commit errors because if you are not committing errors, you are not learning.

Be that as it may, it is completely unsatisfactory to rehash those missteps. Many expert stock traders have made a notable number of mistakes in their commerce vocation. The magnificent concept relating to the stock market is that you generally realize when you are correct or wrong. If you are failing cash, at that point you have most likely accomplished something incorrectly. In the long run, if you learn not to continue making similar blunders, you will begin coming up short on them.

It is important for a beginner to realize that they should never rush to make a trade, instead of the remaining patient. Do not itch to spend money, instead save it and use it only when you are completely ready. Utilize a demo account because you will be able to practice for yourself and spot out common mistakes that are likely to be costly. The whole concept of trading demands that it is done in a patient and systematic manner so that different trends can be analyzed.

The novice must always be patient because otherwise, they will lose a lot of money just trying to learn a single concept. Identify the common mistakes that are likely to occur when you begin trading so as to avoid them. If you understand the mistakes that await you, you put yourself in a chance to learn from them and eventually start profiting from your trades.

The following are a highlight of mistakes that novice traders make and might hinder their progress;

1. Lack of Preparation

As you begin trading, you would do well to be prepared. Notwithstanding, a couple of traders play out the persistence before moving quickly into the markets. If you are attempting to dive with the sharks, you improved from the sharks. The market is a natural way of life — the huge fish eat the little fish.

There are only a few books that show you the necessities of trading, so the suggestion is increasing the chances to support you by perusing whatever number as could reasonably be expected. "You shouldn't disparage the time, devotion, and duty it takes to be a fruitful trader. You can't simply stroll into the market with a bunch of cash and hope to remove cash from the experts. If that is the situation, you are betting, not trading."

Dr. Senior concurs that numerous individuals think little of the stuff to achieve success. Without a business college instruction or hands-on preparing with a financial firm, it takes quite a while to experience profits as a trader. While a foundation in financial administrations would have been useful for this profession, once in a while profoundly instructed traders can get up to speed in the specialized examination. The market does not generally produce that way because markets have an immense level of unpredictability. How you work in an air of vulnerability can be significantly more profitable than the sort of examination you use.

2. Do Not Put Emotion into Money

Most people sometimes do not realize that trading is based on factual information and not their emotions. People believe that because they feel a certain way, success should be inevitable because all the signs are right. But the truth is, trading is based on seeking factual information in order to determine different prices. The process of trading certainly is guided by facts rather than emotions. If trade differences with them, many feel they are failing with wellbeing. That is the intent they will, in general, respond so inwardly.

"To keep from being off-base, numerous individuals frequently will let a stock go negative against them. Suppose they put a stop at 30. As it drops to 29, at that point 28, they here and there choose to conflict with their unique trading plan. To keep from selling at a misfortune, they all of a sudden choose to hold as long as possible. That is regularly an excruciating blunder."

Dr. Senior concurs: "If you came into my trading room and sat opposite me, you wouldn't know if I was making $10,000 that day or losing $10,000. I do not demonstrate that much feeling. I'm increasingly worried about the long term results of my trading. It is increasingly fitting to take a gander at your record toward the part of the bargain or year, instead of your day by day results."

It is possible to put emotions aside by developing a regular reading schedule and always ensuring that you remain up to date with the latest trading strategies. When we focus on a specific approach to trading, it becomes factual and this minimizes the chances of losses. It is important to consider the necessity of collecting information in a dedicated manner in order to guarantee success in trading activities. Putting emotions aside aligns with the objective of treating trading like a business to put you in the right trading mindset. Do not just think of it as a pastime activity because it has the propensity of making you a credible income source.

3. Absence of Recordkeeping

There is a reason for the passion most traders show. Senior says: "When you make a trade, everything is going up or down. It can feel like you have no influence over what's going on. By the very idea of purchasing and selling, total outsiders are giving you cash or removing cash, and that can be upsetting."

In order to be more stable, elder prescribes maintaining a comprehensive trading journal. "Each time you enter a trade, print out the chart and record why you entered the trade, regardless of whether it was crucial, specialized, or a tip. Compose the section on the left side and the exit on the correct side." The journal causes you to accomplish two objectives; "The first is to profit. The second is to improve as a trader. You probably won't prevail on the principal objective, however, you should totally prevail on the subsequent objective. You should attempt to improve as a trader after each trade."

Maintaining up-to-date records is a necessity. "Demonstrate to me a trader with great records and I will demonstrate to you a decent trader. Regardless of whether you are losing cash gradually, you are gaining from your errors. I accept cash the board and recordkeeping are considerably more significant than specialized examination — and I'm a person who composed two books on the specialized investigation."

4. Foreseeing Profits

It is not advisable to start foreseeing your profits even before they have checked in. This is because you will be counting your chicks before they hatch and anything can happen during a trade. It is important to remain optimistic, but that should be the extent of it because you must ensure that you remain focused on implementing your plan. Foreseeing profits can give you false hopes and this can be particularly damaging when looking to advance your trading options.

"Give the market a chance to reveal to you what you are going to make. Whenever you state 'I need to... 'You are in a difficult situation. Keep in mind: The market couldn't care less about you."

Getting into the market with an impartial frame of mind is just about right. "My mantra: What is, is. If you are in an upturn, go long. If you are in a downtrend, go short. If you are overbought, hang tight for inversion and go short. If you are oversold, hang tight for inversion and go long."

5. Mechanical Systems Can Be Misleading

You must be wary of the software and other hardware that you use when guiding you to trade. As always, collecting information for yourself is extremely important even if you have machines working to reap information for your benefit. Counter-check everything before making important decisions because machines can also make errors. It is also possible for you to make a wrong setting change and this can easily affect your trade and cause you to experience simultaneous losses.

"Individuals believe that the PC is a substitution for what is between the ears." "They think the crate is going to offer them the response. Many individuals incline toward mechanical trading frameworks that should assume control over the trading for them." "When you quit any pretense of reasoning and investigating," he says, "you are toast. If you are aimlessly following mechanical frameworks to purchase and sell, all things considered, you are uncertain of precisely what you are doing."

6. Learning to Short is Important

On the off chance that you are not familiar with short trading, at that point, you have removed yourself of various beneficial trades, specialists' state. Numerous individuals feel that shorting is not the way to go. Be that as it may, the failure to learn to short increases your chances of risk tremendously. It becomes a necessity for any trader, particularly a beginner to start familiarizing themselves with various techniques of shorting in order to guarantee success in their investments.

"I trust it is basic that traders figure out how to short. It is one of my first leads: Thou Shall Learn How to Short. In view of dread or obliviousness, numerous Americans never figure out how to short in their lifetime. They're apprehensive about boundless risk. However, shorting a stock is not any riskier than going long." Traders should learn the practice first-hand. "You can't hold tight. If the stock goes up, at that point you get out. It is that straightforward."

"The market is a two-way road, and the individual who does not short is feeling the loss of a piece of the game." As stocks will, in general, decrease quicker than going up, shorting might be most appropriate for transient periods. For novices hoping to figure out how to put it in practice, locate a stock that has reduced projections and undercut close to 100 offers.

Learning the basic techniques of shorting will make any beginner trader have more confidence because they will have greater insight into the system. This enables them to understand the specific investments they need to make in order to guarantee success on their trades. Taking advice with regard to this technique is important because there are specific ways in which it is beneficially implemented. Shorting gives a novice trader a tremendous advantage because there are those who have been trading for a long period of time but have not bothered to comprehensively learn about shorting.

7. Specialization Absence

Numerous individuals go into trading since they believe it is a simple vehicle for profiting. For beginners, it can appear to be an overwhelming undertaking to get familiar with the qualities of every security type. Along these lines, it is regularly useful to practice. "When developing traders do not at first have practical experience in some section of the markets, they could be powerless to over-taking part in whatever hot market fragment tags along. Effective trading requires some investment, so it is very useful to be devoted and focused on a specific class."

A majority of trading specialists recommend that you must have some sort of advantage in order to get into a trade. Otherwise, ignore the impulse because you have to put an appropriate plan in place to exploit the available opportunity. What do you realize that will give you some level of conviction? "If you do not have a clue about the response to this inquiry," he proceeds, "at that point, you should not be trading. My answer: I know a couple of things about specialized examination since I composed a couple of books on it. I can investigate charts with some level of profundity. I've been prepared to perceive what is genuine and what is a dream. Also, I'm incredibly restrained."

8. Inappropriate Timing

When looking to get into specific markets or trade-specific stocks, you must ensure that your timing is right to avoid unnecessary costs or even being overcharged for certain resources. It is not always possible to get a trade at the right time, but consistently anticipating the trade after spending numerous hours of practice will help you sharpen your skills.

"Brilliant individuals get in too early and apprentices get in too late. If you hold up long enough, a stock may begin to resemble a smart thought, yet by then it is regularly too late." Having a sense of consistency is extremely important in guaranteeing success. This is because you learn different tricks that you might not otherwise see, and you are able to make choices based on emerging information. Have a sense of timing as it is the most important thing for you to consider when looking to capitalize on a trade. Most experts agree that some of their most successful Tradings were based on good timing and this enabled them to get an advantage in the market. Exploiting limits could enable traders to all the more likely to deal with their portfolio risk.

When looking for trade openings, utilize a one-year time period in light of the fact that there is a great deal of information focuses. Deel is cognizant about planning his entrance and leaves focuses. "It is those developments here and there that profit. I need to feel positive about a stock three days after I got it. If not, something isn't right."

9. Setting Inappropriate Stops

When you set inappropriate stops, you set yourself up for failure because you will end up incurring a greater level of losses than you were willing to incur. Your stop-loss is your guarantee that you reduce the risk of making losses when trading. Failure to recognize the importance of this and the trade will move in a disadvantageous direction and will keep making losses if you are not available to stop it immediately. You must use your pivot point or even software to ensure your stops are appropriate.

"You spot stops as indicated by what the market is letting you know, for example, backing and opposition levels," he says, "not as per benefit objectives. The market couldn't care less how a lot of cash you have to make." Deel says that right off the bat in his vocation, he was continually stopped out ahead of schedule, generally more than half the time. "What I found was the market will in general move inside a specific range under typical conditions."

"Presently, when I place a stop, I let the stock's conduct, or standard deviation, reveal to me where the best stop arrangements are. When I let the stock disclose to me where to put the stop, I get stopped out just about 20% of the time."

It is necessary to do the math by yourself in order to know exactly when to set appropriate stops. If you ignore your stops, you ignore your one sure-fire risk averting strategy. You should deeply respect the importance of setting appropriate stops when trading because it can make all the difference in determining whether you have the capital to trade or not. Stops should be calculated using the software, but you can also calculate by hand if necessary and is important for novices so that they can understand the entire process. These are one of those elements of math that traders cannot avoid because of the impact it can have on their success. Finding and setting appropriate stops ensures that there is less chance of losing money during a trade. "You can decide a stock's high and low runs and what it can move dependent on standard deviation and probabilities."

10. Not Calculating a Stock's Risk-Reward Ratio

The risk-reward ratio is extremely important when looking to benefit from stock trading. Most novice traders do not take this into consideration, instead of looking for the trendiest stocks and putting all their money into it. There is nothing wrong when you use a tried and tested method, but you must also consider the level of money you are outing in and the reward you are getting. If you are putting some thousands of dollars to reap rewards in the hundreds of dollars, you might want o to consider your risk. As much as this might be a 'safe' trade with seemingly minimal risk, there is also a chance that the trade can turn on its head.

Therefore, carefully consider the risk-reward ratio as it will dictate the movement of the trade-in every manner and ensure that you can profit. Always be considerate of the amount of money you are outing in a trade because it will make all the difference in determining the sort of risk levels you are operating on. Higher risk levels guarantee higher rewards, but it is a necessity to ensure that it is a risk you can take rather than just following trends. Make sure to do your research comprehensively before making any decisions.

"Each stock is a turkey until demonstrated else," he says. "This is a piece of the screening procedure of a stock." It is necessary to be very careful about the deals you make as you seek to make profits. "I've sat by extraordinary traders who see an ideal arrangement however not the risk-compensate. They get in, and it switches. If I'm going to risk a dollar on a stock, I need to appraise that I can make $2.50 or more before I make the trade. Else, I proceed onward to the following stock."

Chapter 13: Day Trading

Putting trade after trade for the duration of the day, effectively monitoring each development of the market, and making quick cash is, for the most part, energizing parts of day trading. You can be in and out of trade inside only 5 to 15 minutes. Whenever effective, seeing that you caused several dollars in merely minutes to can give an adrenaline surge like no other.

Day trading may likewise give you preferred influence over holding positions overnight (as in swing trading). At the hour of this composition, day trading stocks can give you 4:1 influence as long as you meet certain criteria.

Day trading additionally furnishes you with another kind of influence, which is that since you are trading so as often as possible, you can utilize a similar capital in your record to make numerous trades in a brief timeframe.

Probably the best advantage of day trading is that you maintain a strategic distance from medium-term risk. Medium-term risk alludes to the way that when you hold a situation overnight, your cash is presented to major surprising moves while the market is shut and you are dozing. Such unforeseen emotional moves might be brought about off guard, political, or military news in your nation or another.

These emotional moves medium-term might be brought about by really terrible news, or just gossipy tidbits, or a difference in slant about a stock, sector, or industry. These moves appear as holes — significantly different opening costs than where the markets shut the day preceding — on your chart and can hop your stops, giving a gigantic misfortune to you when you get up the following morning.

A stop is a request you spot to be filled at a specific cost if the market betrays your trade; bouncing your stops happens when the market holes to a value that is past where you put in your stop request.

A stop is regularly called a defensive stop since it is utilized as a defensive measure with the aim of setting the level at which you need to leave a trade that is not going your direction. Thusly, you are endeavoring to constrain your risk in the trade.

Chapter 14: Fundamental & Technical Analysis

When making sense of what to do in the investment world, most experts utilize one of two essential ways to deal with stock trading: major examination and specialized investigation (many utilize a blend of the two). The two methodologies are utilized in various markets extending from the stock market to items. The principal differences between key investigation and specialized examination are quite straightforward:

The principal examination goes into the financial aspects of the organization itself, for example, deals and benefit information, just as outside factors influencing it, for example, legislative issues, guidelines, and industry patterns.

Specialized investigation attempts to comprehend where a stock's cost is going dependent on market conduct as prove in its market measurements (introduced in charts, cost, and trading volume information). The specialized examination does not attempt to make sense of the value of an investment; it is utilized to make sense of where the cost of that stock or investment is drifting.

The most effective method to join key and specialized examination for useful stock contributing

Key investigation causes you to comprehend what to contribute (or trade or hypothesize) in, though specialized examination guides you with respect to when to do it. Since markets rhythmic movement, the specialized examination can enable you to spot okay indicates either enter or leave a trade. Specialized examination, in this manner, causes you to stack the deck somewhat more to support you. Taking into account how markets have been going recently, each and every piece makes a difference.

Mixing the two ways to deal with some degree has been finished with progress. Clearly, if the crucial and the specialized factors bolster your choice, at that point the opportunity for a beneficial trade has all the more taking the plunge. How does this mix happen?

For a model, take a gander at the ideas of oversold and overbought. If you are taking a gander at purchasing a stock (or other investment) since you believe it is a solid investment however you do not know about when to get, you need to take a gander at the specialized information. If the information reveals to you that it has been oversold, it is a decent time to purchase.

Oversold just implies that the market was excessively extraordinary in selling that specific investment during a specific timeframe.

The specialized terms oversold and overbought have a parallel to key terms, for example, underestimated and exaggerated. Since the crucial examination is a noteworthy piece of a way of thinking alluded to as worth contributing, the ideas bode well

Similarly as putting resources into an underestimated stock is normally a smart thought, so is purchasing a stock that has been oversold. It is intelligent to assume that an oversold stock is underestimated (taking everything into account). Obviously, different terms (overbought and exaggerated) can likewise keep running couple.

Then again, the basics can enable a specialized examiner to settle on a superior trading choice. State that a specialized investigator has a gainful position in a specific stock called Getting near a Cliff Corp. (GNAC). If the specialized indicators are turning bearish and the new quarterly income report for GNAC demonstrates a significantly lower benefit, at that point selling GNAC's stock is most likely a smart thought.

The expert's tools for stock investigation

When you fold up your sleeves and get into the specialized investigation, what will you manage? It relies upon what sort of specialized investigator you are. In the specialized investigation, there are two subcategories: the individuals who transcendently use charts (these professionals are called . . .

chartists!) and the individuals who overwhelmingly use information, (for example, cost and volume information). Obviously, numerous specialists utilize a blend of both:

Charts: Charts are the flawless pictures that diagram value developments, (for example, chart designs).

Information: Data incorporates cost and volume data (alongside specialized and conduct indicators got from it).

Specialized investigators do not take a gander at the essentials since they accept that the marketplace (as delineated in the charts, cost, and volume information) as of now consider the basics.

Chapter 15: The Right Trading Mindset

One of the most important things any trader can have is the right trading mindset. This refers to the ability to remain cool and collected every day of the week. Trading stocks is done successfully by those who understand the essence of remaining calm at any given situation in order to carefully monitor something within their proximity.

It is important to understand that enduring surprises time and again will increase your chances of incurring losses when stock trading. You must remain calm and collected, developing a trading mindset that eventually dictates different patterns of your life.

For instance, you might have to start waking up late at night or in the early hours of the morning in order to follow up on investment. Also, you might have to choose entirely new reading material from your normal information sources, changing the nature and composition of information that you absorb.

Either way, learning to have a positive mindset is pivotal in ensuring that you can attain any kind of success when you start trading. It is necessary to point out that inspiration will always come from within yourself so never go looking for it too far.

Guideline 1: Utilize Technology

Most people underestimate the power of technology in the modern world when it comes to driving different fundamental aspects of life. Technology has been responsible for massive changes in terms of developments and spreading information. You should utilize every bit of technology available to you to somehow ease the process of trading. You should be able to acquire information on the stocks you are interested in with relative ease because of the technology access available to you. There are better methods of communication today than in the past, information moves much faster than in the past and it is possible to make the entire world into a small global online village through social media.

Therefore, there is no excuse not to search for software that and guide you on setting pivot points, stop-losses and even entry points. There are different types of technology that you can utilize in order to get you in the right trading mindset. This way, you can focus on other fundamental aspects of trading while still ensuring that profitability is a guarantee. It is amazing how simple technology works to put you just in the right frame of mind to handle specific challenges that face you as you trade.

Guideline 2: Always Use a Stop-loss

In case you are not familiar with the importance of a stop-loss, this prevents you from making losses when a trade starts making losses. It limits the loss cap for your money, ensuring that you exit a trade just as you hit the stop-loss level. This has the disadvantage of missing out in case the trade suddenly changes and witnesses the boom that you were anticipating. Either way, a stop loss will enable you to be in the right trading mindset because you will not always be fidgety about losing a large amount of money on a single trade.

It will be possible to save your funds for a future trade by relying on a stop-loss even if the trade was to change and start moving into a profitable position. Patience is key when trading and this is epitomized by a stop-loss. A trade that is unstable can easily make you massive losses, so being cautious about the value movements of the trade is critical for success. A stop loss is a necessary risk-tackling measure that you must make particularly if you have immediate short-term goals that must be achieved for the success of the trade.

Guideline 3: Become a Student

A quick way of becoming successful is becoming a student of the very markets you intend to trade-in. At first, make small and few trades, listening to advice and gauging the market with the knowledge that you already have. There is never a time to stop learning because even if you achieve short-term success, massive losses can easily await you in the near future. Do not underestimate the value of continuously learning because if you observe closely, you will realize that even the expert traders take some time out to learn for themselves.

There are various ways you can become a student; for instance, you can work under the apprenticeship of a master. This does not mean that they set up a trading account, you must show your own commitment by setting up an even trying a trade for yourself. Thereafter, ask a professional trader that you might know of to teach you the ropes of trading so that you can also profit. You can also identify stock market websites that specialize in providing news and other trading-related facts that will help you develop a trading routine and, eventually the right trading mindset.

Guideline 4: A Plan is Important

There is nothing more important than having the right trading plan because, without it, you can never be in the right trading mindset for success. A plan identifies your objectives and the methodology you will use when approaching different challenges. On the off chance that you want to identify your risks, then this makes an important element of the plan you intend to implement.

Remember that you must set everything you want to do in pen or paper or even on an Excel worksheet. Identify the main aspects of trade you want to implement and take into careful consideration the resources you have. One of the most significant parts of the trading plan is the element of time because you must plan for it in an appropriate manner. Remember that time is everything and once lost, it is impossible to recover.

A proper plan will set you in the right mood for trading because you will be able to envision whatever you want to implement. You will have foreseen some problems and usually, this is enough to ensure success. Therefore, take some time and plan before launching into your first trade.

Guideline 5: Identify Rest Periods Beforehand

As much as it is important to constantly stay on the loop as you will soon discover when you start trading, having a rest is equally important. You might want to continuously trade and make money because of the ongoing opportunities right before you. However, what is more, important is investing in time for yourself as well as family and friends because it makes all the difference in having the right trading mindset. When you overwork yourself, you can be sure that you will never be in the right trading mindset.

Have a conversation with the people close to you; understand what is going on in their lives. This is just as important to you as the trading process and you must always recognize those who are close and around you. Set limits for the time you trade and do not bog yourself down in front of a computer screen attempting to profit on a late trade; if it is time for bed, it is time for bed. You must recognize the importance of giving yourself a rest because you can only produce to your best when you are fresh and full of energy to go.

Guideline 6: Make Sure Trading is a Business to You

Avoid constantly taking money out of your account just to spend it on something simple and unnecessary when one of your trades has come right. Instead, plow the money back into the trade and identify your losses or profits. Try to use as much money as possible in order to spread different trades and minimize the risk of incurring losses. When you think of your trades just like a business and the thing to put food on your plate, then you are on the right track to achieving success.

Guideline 7: Make Sure Your Trading Practices are Reasonable

If you have $2,000 in your trading account, do not trade it all away; instead, look for minimalist strategies that will allow you to trade on multiple exchanges and try to profit. This way, you spread the risk through several trades and increase your income when a majority of them come right. You will not be pressured for all your trades to go right because only a few from your choices will be sufficient to cover your losses and produce a profit, as well.

Guideline 8: Planning for Trading Capital is Important

When you understand the importance of your trading capital, you are able to make trading a continuous practice and constantly profiting. Just as your trades need to be reasonable, ensure that you have a back-up for your trading capital for the same amount. These are some of the things that make trading quite difficult and must be considered in order to provoke some success. Your trading capital will always give you an advantage when you make losses because you will have gained crucial information on a specific market and able to turn to your substitute capital in order to make profits.

Guideline 9: Have a Trading Methodology

When you have a consistent method of trading, it empowers you to make the right decision in terms of your investments in the stocks. This certainly sets you in the right mindset because you can identify favorable spots in the market and utilize them appropriately. A right trading mindset is enhanced by an appropriate approach to trading that you have developed and is suitable for utilizing your strengths to guarantee success. A trading methodology sets you in the right frame of mind for trading because you will be able to view most of the challenges you encounter in a positive way.

Guideline 10: Do Not Risk Too Much

Most people end up risking much more than they really can afford to, and this leads to their demise. You have heard of stories where consistent traders who were once making a living from the stock market now completely out of cash and living in dire conditions. Most people usually use these stories as an example to keep from trading, but the truth is that you should only bite off what you can chew.

If you put your entire life savings in a trade without a back-up, it will be your fault if you lose all the money and have to start a new life. Never risk more than you need to because you should always trade within your limits to grow. It is the only sure way of achieving success because the benefits of trade will not come immediately, but to those who are patient enough to wait.

Conclusion

Thank you for making it through to the end of *Stock Trading for Beginners*, let's hope it was informative and able to provide you with all of the tools you need to achieve your goals whatever they may be.

The next step is to like us on social media and spread the word about the helpfulness of the book.

Finally, if you found this book useful in any way, a review on Amazon is always appreciated!

www.ingramcontent.com/pod-product-compliance
Lightning Source LLC
Chambersburg PA
CBHW070347220526
45467CB00001B/276